America's
Favorite Brand Name
RECIPES

Bradford
Press

Pictured on the front cover *(clockwise from top left):* Layered Pasta Casserole *(page 133)*, European Mocha Fudge Cake *(page 165)*, Shrimp and Pepper Bisque *(page 80)* and Cheesy Chimichangas *(page 140)*.
Pictured on the back cover *(top to bottom):* Fluffy Peanut Butter Pie *(page 170)*, Saucy Asparagus Casserole *(page 93)* and Chicken with Grilled Pineapple Salsa *(page 144)*.

ISBN-13: 978-1-4508-2676-1
ISBN-10: 1-4508-2676-8

Manufactured in China.

8 7 6 5 4 3 2 1

Microwave Cooking: Microwave ovens vary in wattage. Use the cooking times as guidelines and check for doneness before adding more time.

Preparation/Cooking Times: Preparation times are based on the approximate amount of time required to assemble the recipe before cooking, baking, chilling or serving. These times include preparation steps such as measuring, chopping and mixing. The fact that some preparations and cooking can be done simultaneously is taken into account. Preparation of optional ingredients and serving suggestions is not included.

Publications International, Ltd.

contents

· · · · ·

acknowledgments

· · · · ·

Alouette® Spreadable Cheese, Alouette® Baby Brie®, Alouette® Crème Spreadable, Chavrie®, Saladena®

American Lamb Board

BelGioioso® Cheese Inc.

Bob Evans®

California Tree Fruit Agreement

California Walnut Board

Campbell Soup Company

Cream of Wheat® Cereal

Del Monte Foods

Dole Food Company, Inc.

Domino® Foods, Inc.

Duncan Hines® and Moist Deluxe® are registered trademarks of Pinnacle Foods Corp.

EAGLE BRAND®

Filippo Berio® Olive Oil

Fisher® Nuts

Florida Department of Citrus

Grandma's®, A Division of B&G Foods, Inc.

Heinz North America

The Hershey Company

Hillshire Farm®

Hormel Foods, LLC

Jarden Consumer Solutions, Inc.

JOLLY TIME® Pop Corn

The Kahlúa® Liqueur trademark is used under permission from The Kahlúa Company, Purchase NY

Kraft Foods Global, Inc.

© Mars, Incorporated 2010

MASTERFOODS USA

McIlhenny Company (TABASCO® brand Pepper Sauce)

National Honey Board

National Turkey Federation

National Watermelon Promotion Board

Nestlé USA

Newman's Own, Inc.®

North Dakota Wheat Commission

Ortega®, A Division of B&G Foods, Inc.

Polaner®, A Division of B&G Foods, Inc.

The Quaker® Oatmeal Kitchens

Reckitt Benckiser Inc.

Recipes courtesy of the Reynolds Kitchens

Riviana Foods Inc.

Sargento® Foods Inc.

SeaPak Shrimp Company®

StarKist®

The Sugar Association, Inc.

Reprinted with permission of Sunkist Growers, Inc. All Rights Reserved.

Sun•Maid® Growers of California

Unilever

USA Rice Federation®

U.S. Highbush Blueberry Council

Watkins Incorporated

Wisconsin Milk Marketing Board

appetizers & snacks

appetizers & snacks

· · · · ·

cool veggie pizza appetizer

Makes 32 servings

2 cans (8 ounces each) refrigerated crescent dinner rolls
1 package (8 ounces) PHILADELPHIA® Cream Cheese, softened
½ cup MIRACLE WHIP® Dressing
1 teaspoon dill weed
½ teaspoon onion salt
1 cup broccoli florets
1 cup chopped green bell pepper
1 cup chopped seeded tomato
¼ cup chopped red onion

PREHEAT oven to 375°F. Separate dough into 4 rectangles. Press onto bottom and up side of 15×10×1-inch baking pan to form crust.

BAKE 11 to 13 minutes or until golden brown; cool.

MIX cream cheese, dressing, dill and onion salt until well blended. Spread over crust; top with remaining ingredients. Refrigerate. Cut into squares.

Prep Time: 20 minutes plus refrigerating
Bake Time: 11 to 13 minutes

hot cheesy chili dip

hot cheesy chili dip

Makes about 5 cups

1 pound lean ground beef
½ cup chopped onion
1 package (1 pound) pasteurized process cheese spread with jalapeño pepper, cut into cubes
1 can (15 ounces) kidney beans, drained
1 bottle (12 ounces) HEINZ® Chili Sauce
¼ cup chopped fresh parsley
Tortilla chips or crackers

In large saucepan, cook beef and onion until onion is tender; drain. Stir in cheese, beans and chili sauce; heat, stirring until cheese is melted. Stir in parsley. Serve warm with tortilla chips or crackers.

Tip: When shopping for lean ground beef, pay attention to the fat content rather than the cut (sirloin, round or chuck). A higher percentage indicates leaner meat (92% is leaner than 85%).

chipotle-spiced nuts

Makes 1 pound

1 pound mixed nuts
4 tablespoons butter, melted
2 tablespoons ORTEGA® Chipotle Taco Seasoning Mix
1 tablespoon light brown sugar

PREHEAT oven to 325°F. Toss nuts, butter, seasoning mix and brown sugar in large bowl until well combined.

SPREAD nut mixture on baking pan. Bake 20 minutes, stirring after 10 minutes. Serve warm, if desired. To store, allow to cool, then place in airtight container for up to 2 weeks.

Serving Suggestion: Try sprinkling these nuts over your favorite ice cream for a flavorful "hot" and cold dessert.

Note: For gift-giving to friends and family, pack these deliciously spicy nuts in a decorative tin can. You can share the recipe on a gift tag, too!

guacamole

Makes about 2 cups

2 avocados, mashed
¼ cup red salsa (mild or hot, according to taste)
3 tablespoons NEWMAN'S OWN® Salad Dressing
2 tablespoons lime or lemon juice
1 clove garlic, finely minced
Salt and black pepper

Combine all ingredients and mix well. Chill for 1 to 2 hours tightly covered. Serve with tortilla chips.

beef empanadas

Makes 9 servings

1 tablespoon olive oil
3 tablespoons finely chopped onion
1 clove garlic, minced
¼ pound ground beef
2 tablespoons chopped pimiento-stuffed green olives
2 tablespoons raisins
2 tablespoons ketchup
1 tablespoon chopped fresh parsley
½ teaspoon ground cumin
1 sheet frozen puff pastry (half of 17¼-ounce package), thawed
1 egg yolk

1. Preheat oven to 400°F. Line baking sheet with parchment paper.

2. Heat oil in large skillet over medium-high heat. Add onion and garlic; cook and stir 2 minutes. Add beef; cook 6 to 8 minutes, stirring to break up meat. Drain fat. Add olives, raisins, ketchup, parsley and cumin; cook and stir 2 minutes.

3. Roll out pastry into 12-inch square on lightly floured surface. Cut into nine 4-inch squares. Place rounded tablespoonful beef mixture in center of each square. Fold over to form triangle; seal edges with fork. Place on prepared baking sheet. Bake 18 to 20 minutes or until golden brown.

Tip: When using only one sheet of puff pastry, wrap the remaining sheet in plastic wrap or foil and return it to the freezer. Thaw the pastry in the refrigerator for the best results.

edamame frittata

Makes 4 servings

2 tablespoons olive oil
½ cup frozen shelled edamame
⅓ cup frozen corn
1 shallot, chopped
5 eggs
¾ teaspoon Italian seasoning
½ teaspoon salt
½ teaspoon black pepper
¼ cup chopped green onions
½ cup crumbled goat cheese

1. Preheat broiler. Heat oil in large broilerproof skillet over medium-high heat. Add edamame, corn and shallot; cook and stir 6 to 8 minutes or until shallot is brown.

2. Meanwhile, beat eggs, seasoning, salt and pepper in medium bowl. Stir in green onions. Pour egg mixture over vegetables in skillet. Sprinkle with cheese. Cook over medium heat 5 to 7 minutes or until eggs are set on bottom, lifting up mixture to allow uncooked portion to flow underneath.

3. Broil 6 inches from heat 1 minute or until top is puffy and golden. Loosen frittata from skillet with spatula; slide onto small platter. Cut into wedges.

beef empanadas

mini taco cups

Makes 24 appetizers

- 24 wonton wrappers
- 1 pound lean ground beef
- 1 packet (1.25 ounces) ORTEGA® Taco Seasoning Mix
- ½ cup plus 2 tablespoons ORTEGA® Thick & Chunky Salsa, divided
- 1 cup (4 ounces) shredded Mexican-blend cheese
  Additional ORTEGA® Thick & Chunky Salsa
  Sour cream (optional)
  B&G® Sliced Black Olives (optional)

PREHEAT oven to 425°F. Coat 24 mini muffin cups with nonstick cooking spray. Press wonton wrappers into cups.

COOK and stir beef in medium skillet over medium heat until browned. Drain excess fat and discard.

STIR in seasoning mix and 2 tablespoons salsa. Spoon mixture evenly into wonton cups. Top evenly with remaining ½ cup salsa and cheese.

BAKE 8 minutes or until wontons are golden brown. Serve immediately with additional salsa. Garnish with sour cream and olives, if desired.

Prep Time: 15 minutes
Start-to-Finish Time: 25 minutes

Tip: Wonton wrappers can be found in Asian markets or in the Asian specialties aisle of most supermarkets.

italian sub crostini

Makes 12 crostini

- 1 (6-inch) loaf French bread, cut into ½-inch slices
  Olive oil
- 1 ball (8 ounces) fresh mozzarella cheese, cut into 12 slices
- 8 ounces sliced prosciutto

1. Preheat oven to 400°F. Brush bread slices with oil. Place on ungreased baking sheet. Bake 5 minutes or until crisp.

2. Place one slice mozzarella on each toast. Cut prosciutto into thin slivers; sprinkle over cheese. Bake 3 minutes or until cheese is melted. Serve immediately.

everything ham dip

Makes about 2 cups

- 1 (3-ounce) package cream cheese, softened
- ½ cup sour cream
- 1 tablespoon sherry
- 1 (5-ounce) can HORMEL® chunk ham, drained and flaked
- 2 tablespoons chopped water chestnuts
- 2 tablespoons minced onion
- ½ teaspoon dried dill weed
- 3 slices HORMEL® bacon, cooked and crumbled
- 3 tablespoons finely chopped pecans
  Melba toast, if desired

Beat cream cheese until light and fluffy. Add sour cream and sherry. Beat until smooth. Stir in ham, water chestnuts, onion and dill weed. Cover and refrigerate until chilled, about 1 hour. Stir in bacon and pecans just before serving. Serve with melba toast.

slow-cooked mini pulled pork bites

Makes 16 mini sandwiches

- 1 can (10¾ ounces) CAMPBELL'S® Condensed Tomato Soup
- ½ cup packed brown sugar
- ¼ cup cider vinegar
- 1 teaspoon garlic powder
- 4 pounds boneless pork shoulder
- 1 package (13.9 ounces) PEPPERIDGE FARM® Soft Country Style Dinner Rolls
- Hot pepper sauce (optional)

Slow Cooker Directions

1. Stir the soup, brown sugar, vinegar and garlic powder in a 6-quart slow cooker. Add the pork and turn to coat.

2. Cover and cook on LOW for 6 to 7 hours* or until the pork is fork-tender.

3. Remove the pork from the cooker to a cutting board and let stand for 10 minutes. Using 2 forks, shred the pork. Return the pork to the cooker.

4. Divide the pork mixture among the rolls. Serve with the hot pepper sauce, if desired.

*Or on HIGH for 4 to 5 hours.

slow-cooked mini pulled pork bites

hot "crab" and artichoke dip

Makes 6 to 8 servings

- 1 (8-ounce) package cream cheese, softened
- ½ cup mayonnaise
- ½ cup shredded Cheddar cheese
- ¼ cup CREAM OF WHEAT® Hot Cereal (Instant, 1-minute, 2½-minute or 10-minute cook time), uncooked
- 1 teaspoon TRAPPEY'S® Red Devil™ Cayenne Pepper Sauce
- 1 teaspoon Worcestershire sauce
- 1 teaspoon Chesapeake seasoning
- 1 (9-ounce) jar artichoke hearts, drained and coarsely chopped
- 8 ounces pasteurized surimi (imitation crabmeat), coarsely chopped
- 1 teaspoon ground paprika
- Vegetables, crackers or tortilla chips (optional)

1. Preheat oven to 350°F. Stir cream cheese in medium mixing bowl until smooth. Add mayonnaise, Cheddar cheese, Cream of Wheat, pepper sauce, Worcestershire sauce and Chesapeake seasoning; mix well. Fold in artichoke hearts and surimi.

2. Pour into 1-quart casserole dish. Sprinkle on paprika. Bake 30 minutes. Serve warm with vegetables, crackers or tortilla chips, if desired.

Prep Time: 15 minutes
Start-to-Finish Time: 45 minutes

apricot brie en croûte

apricot brie en croûte

Makes 6 servings

1 sheet frozen puff pastry (half of 17¼-ounce package)
1 round (8 ounces) Brie cheese
¼ cup apricot preserves

1. Unfold puff pastry and thaw 20 minutes on lightly floured surface. Preheat oven to 400°F. Line baking sheet with parchment paper.

2. Roll out puff pastry to 12-inch square. Place Brie in center of square; spread preserves over top of Brie.

3. Gather up edges of puff pastry and bring together over center of Brie, covering cheese entirely. Pinch and twist pastry edges together to seal. Transfer to prepared baking sheet.

4. Bake 20 to 25 minutes or until golden brown. (If top of pastry browns too quickly, cover loosely with foil.) Serve warm.

Variation: For added flavor and texture, sprinkle 2 tablespoons sliced almonds over the preserves in step 2.

tuna in crispy wonton cups

- 18 wonton skins, each 3¼ inches square
- Butter or olive oil cooking spray
- 1 (2.6-ounce) STARKIST Flavor Fresh Pouch® Tuna (Albacore or Chunk Light)
- ⅓ cup cold cooked orzo (rice-shaped pasta) or cooked rice
- ¼ cup southwestern ranch-style vegetable dip with jalapeños or other sour cream dip
- ¼ cup drained pimiento-stuffed green olives, chopped
- 3 tablespoons sweet pickle relish, drained
- Paprika, for garnish
- Parsley sprigs, for garnish

Cut wontons into circles with 3-inch round cookie cutter. Spray miniature muffin pan with cooking spray. Place one circle in each muffin cup; press to sides to mold wonton to cup. Spray each wonton with cooking spray. Bake in 350°F oven 6 to 8 minutes or until golden brown; set aside.

In small bowl, gently mix tuna, orzo, dip, olives and relish. Refrigerate filling until ready to serve. Remove wonton cups from muffin pan. Use rounded teaspoon to fill each cup; garnish with paprika and parsley.

Prep Time: 20 minutes

Tip: These cups can be made one day ahead; store in airtight container. Reheat in 350°F oven 1 to 2 minutes to recrisp.

hummus

- 1 can (about 15 ounces) chickpeas, rinsed and drained
- 3 tablespoons lemon juice
- 4½ teaspoons tahini*
- ½ teaspoon ground cumin
- ¼ teaspoon salt
- ¼ teaspoon black pepper
- ½ cup chopped seeded tomato
- ⅓ cup chopped red onion
- ⅓ cup chopped celery
- ⅓ cup chopped seeded cucumber
- ⅓ cup chopped green or red bell pepper
- 2 pita bread rounds

*Tahini, a thick paste made from ground sesame seeds, is available in the international foods section of major supermarkets, Middle Eastern markets or health food stores.

1. Combine chickpeas, lemon juice, tahini, cumin, salt and black pepper in food processor or blender; process until smooth. If mixture is too thick to spread, add water until desired consistency is reached.

2. Spoon chickpea mixture into serving bowl. Top with tomato, onion, celery, cucumber and bell pepper.

3. Preheat broiler. Split pitas horizontally in half to form 4 rounds. Cut each round into 6 wedges. Place on baking sheet; broil 3 minutes or until crisp.

4. Serve Hummus with warm pita wedges.

apple salsa with cilantro and lime

Makes 2 cups

1 cup finely chopped unpeeled red apples
¼ cup finely chopped red onion
¼ cup minced Anaheim pepper
½ jalapeño pepper,* seeded and minced (optional)
2 tablespoons lime juice
1 teaspoon chopped fresh cilantro
¼ teaspoon black pepper
⅛ teaspoon salt
Tortilla chips

Jalapeño peppers can sting and irritate the skin, so wear rubber gloves when handling peppers and do not touch your eyes.

1. Combine apples, onion, Anaheim pepper, jalapeño pepper, if desired, lime juice, cilantro, black pepper and salt in large bowl; mix well. Cover; refrigerate at least 30 minutes or overnight.

2. Serve with tortilla chips.

festive nachos

Makes 4 servings

5 ounces tortilla chips
3 cups Mexican blend shredded cheese
2 cups *French's*® French Fried Onions
1 cup chopped plum tomatoes
½ cup sliced black olives

Microwave Directions

1. Layer chips, cheese, French Fried Onions, tomatoes and olives on microwave-safe plate. Microwave on HIGH 2 to 3 minutes or until cheese melts.

2. Serve with salsa and prepared guacamole if desired.

asian honey-tea grilled prawns

Makes 4 servings

1½ pounds medium raw shrimp, peeled and deveined
Salt
2 green onions, thinly sliced

Marinade
1 cup brewed double-strength orange-spice tea, cooled
¼ cup honey
¼ cup rice vinegar
¼ cup soy sauce
1 tablespoon finely chopped fresh ginger
½ teaspoon ground black pepper

In plastic bag, combine marinade ingredients. Remove ½ cup marinade; set aside for dipping sauce. Add shrimp to marinade in bag, turning to coat. Close bag securely and marinate in refrigerator 30 minutes or up to 12 hours.

Remove shrimp from marinade; discard marinade. Thread shrimp onto 8 skewers, dividing evenly. Grill over medium coals 4 to 6 minutes or until shrimp turn pink and are just firm to the touch, turning once. Season with salt, as desired.

Meanwhile, prepare dipping sauce by placing reserved ½ cup marinade in small saucepan. Bring to a boil over medium-high heat. Boil 3 to 5 minutes or until slightly reduced. Stir in green onions.

Favorite recipe from **National Honey Board**

apple salsa with cilantro and lime

raspberry-balsamic glazed meatballs

raspberry-balsamic glazed meatballs

Makes about 32 meatballs

1 bag (32 ounces) frozen fully
   cooked meatballs
1 cup raspberry preserves
3 tablespoons sugar
3 tablespoons balsamic vinegar
1 tablespoon plus 1½ teaspoons
   Worcestershire sauce
¼ teaspoon red pepper flakes
1 tablespoon grated fresh ginger

Slow Cooker Directions
1. Coat slow cooker with nonstick
cooking spray. Add meatballs.

2. Combine preserves, sugar, vinegar,
Worcestershire sauce and red pepper
flakes in small microwavable bowl.
Microwave on HIGH 45 seconds; stir.
Microwave 15 seconds or until melted.
Reserve ½ cup preserves mixture. Pour
remaining mixture over meatballs; toss
to coat. Cover; cook on LOW 5 hours or
on HIGH 2½ hours.

3. *Turn slow cooker to HIGH.* Stir in
ginger and reserved ½ cup preserves
mixture. Cook, uncovered, 15 to
20 minutes or until thickened slightly,
stirring occasionally.

cinnamon popcorn

Makes 18 cups

- 10 cups air-popped popcorn (½ cup unpopped)
- 1½ cups (7 ounces) coarsely chopped pecans
- ¾ cup granulated sugar
- ¾ cup packed light brown sugar
- ½ cup light corn syrup
- 3 tablespoons *Frank's® RedHot®* Original Cayenne Pepper Sauce
- 2 tablespoons honey
- 6 tablespoons (¾ stick) unsalted butter, at room temperature, cut into thin pats
- 1 tablespoon ground cinnamon

1. Preheat oven to 250°F. Place popcorn and pecans in 5-quart ovenproof bowl or Dutch oven. Bake 15 minutes.

2. Combine sugars, corn syrup, *Frank's RedHot* Sauce and honey in 2-quart saucepan. Bring to a full boil over medium-high heat, stirring just until sugars dissolve. Boil about 6 to 8 minutes or until soft crack stage (290°F on candy thermometer). *Do not stir.* Remove from heat.

3. Gradually add butter and cinnamon to sugar mixture, stirring gently until well blended. Pour over popcorn, tossing to coat evenly.* Spread popcorn mixture on greased baking sheets, using two forks. Cool completely. Break into bite-size pieces. Store in airtight container up to 2 weeks.

If popcorn mixture sets too quickly, return to oven to rewarm. Popcorn mixture may be shaped into 3-inch balls while warm, if desired.

Prep Time: 15 minutes
Cook Time: 8 to 10 minutes

two tomato-kalamata crostini

Makes 20 servings

- 8 sun-dried tomatoes (not packed in oil)
- 1 French bread baguette, cut into 20 (¼-inch-thick) slices
- 5 ounces grape tomatoes, chopped
- 12 kalamata olives, pitted and finely chopped
- 2 teaspoons cider vinegar
- 1½ teaspoons dried basil
- 1 teaspoon extra virgin olive oil
- ⅛ teaspoon salt
- 1 clove garlic, halved crosswise

1. Preheat oven to 350°F. Place sun-dried tomatoes in small bowl; cover with boiling water. Let stand 10 minutes. Drain; chop tomatoes.

2. Place bread slices on large baking sheet. Bake 10 minutes or until edges are golden brown. Cool on wire rack.

3. Meanwhile, combine sun-dried tomatoes, grape tomatoes, olives, vinegar, basil, oil and salt in medium bowl; mix well.

4. Rub bread slices with garlic. Top each bread slice with 1 tablespoon tomato mixture.

two tomato-kalamata crostini

zesty crab cakes with red pepper sauce

Makes about 1 dozen crab cakes

½ pound raw medium shrimp,
  shelled and deveined
⅔ cup heavy cream
1 egg white
3 tablespoons *Frank's® RedHot®*
  Original Cayenne Pepper Sauce
1 tablespoon *French's®*
  Worcestershire Sauce
¼ teaspoon seasoned salt
1 pound crabmeat or imitation
  crabmeat, flaked (4 cups)
1 red or yellow bell pepper, minced
2 green onions, minced
¼ cup minced fresh parsley
1½ cups fresh bread crumbs
½ cup corn oil
  Red Pepper Sauce (recipe follows)

1. Place shrimp, cream, egg white,
Frank's RedHot Sauce, Worcestershire
and seasoned salt in food processor.
Process until mixture is puréed.
Transfer to large bowl.

2. Add crabmeat, bell pepper, onions
and parsley. Mix with fork until well
blended.

3. Shape crabmeat mixture into
12 (½-inch-thick) patties, using about
¼ cup mixture for each. Coat both
sides in bread crumbs.

4. Heat oil in large nonstick skillet.
Add crab cakes; cook until browned
on both sides. Drain on paper towels.
Serve with Red Pepper Sauce.

Prep Time: 30 minutes
Cook Time: 15 minutes

red pepper sauce

1 jar (7 ounces) roasted red peppers,
  drained
¼ cup mayonnaise
3 tablespoons *Frank's® RedHot®*
  Original Cayenne Pepper Sauce
2 tablespoons minced onion
1 tablespoon *French's®* Spicy Brown
  Mustard
1 tablespoon minced parsley
1 clove garlic

Place all ingredients in blender or food
processor. Cover; process until smooth.
Makes 1 cup sauce

two cheese pesto dip

Makes 2 cups dip

1 cup light sour cream
½ cup (2 ounces) SARGENTO®
  Shredded Reduced Fat
  Mozzarella Cheese
½ cup light mayonnaise
½ cup finely chopped fresh parsley
¼ cup finely chopped walnuts
2 tablespoons SARGENTO®
  ARTISAN BLENDS™ Shredded
  Parmesan Cheese
1½ teaspoons dried basil leaves *or*
  3 tablespoons minced fresh basil
1 clove garlic, minced

COMBINE all ingredients in medium
bowl. Cover and refrigerate several
hours or overnight. Garnish with whole
walnuts, if desired. Serve with assorted
fresh vegetables.

zesty crab cakes with red pepper sauce

sausage-stuffed mushrooms

Makes 24 appetizers

24 medium mushrooms
2 tablespoons butter, melted
¼ pound bulk pork sausage
1 cup PACE® Picante Sauce
½ cup dry bread crumbs
   Chopped fresh cilantro leaves **or**
   fresh parsley

1. Heat the oven to 425°F. Remove the stems from the mushrooms. Chop enough stems to make **1 cup**. Brush the mushroom caps with the butter and place top-side down in a shallow baking pan.

2. Cook the sausage and the chopped mushroom stems in a 10-inch skillet over medium-high heat until the sausage is well browned, stirring often to break up the meat. Pour off any fat.

3. Add ½ **cup** picante sauce and the bread crumbs to the skillet and mix lightly. Spoon about 1 tablespoon sausage mixture into each mushroom cap.

4. Bake for 10 minutes or until the mushrooms are hot. Top **each** with **1 teaspoon** picante sauce and sprinkle with the cilantro.

sausage-stuffed mushrooms

honey-roasted bridge mix

Makes 4 cups

½ cup honey
2 tablespoons butter or margarine
1 teaspoon ground cinnamon,
   divided
4 cups mixed nuts
2 to 3 tablespoons superfine sugar

Preheat oven to 325°F. Combine honey, butter and ½ teaspoon cinnamon in saucepan. Bring mixture to a boil; cook 2 minutes, stirring constantly. Pour honey mixture over nuts; stir well until nuts are coated. Spread nut mixture onto foil-lined cookie sheet or jelly-roll pan.

Bake 10 to 15 minutes or until nuts are glazed and lightly browned. Do not allow nuts to burn. Cool 20 to 30 minutes; remove from foil. Combine sugar and remaining ½ teaspoon cinnamon; toss with glazed nuts to coat.

Favorite recipe from **National Honey Board**

watermelon kebobs

Makes 6 servings

18 (1-inch) cubes seedless watermelon
6 ounces (1-inch cubes) fat-free
   turkey breast
6 ounces (1-inch cubes) reduced-fat
   Cheddar cheese
6 (6-inch) bamboo skewers

Alternate cubes of watermelon between cubes of turkey and cheese threaded onto each skewer.

Favorite recipe from **National Watermelon Promotion Board**

crispy ranch chicken bites

Makes 6 to 8 servings

Olive oil cooking spray
1 pound boneless skinless chicken breasts
¾ cup ranch dressing
2 cups panko bread crumbs

1. Preheat oven to 375°F. Line baking sheets with foil; spray foil with cooking spray.

2. Cut chicken into 1-inch cubes. Place ranch dressing in small bowl. Spread panko in shallow dish. Dip chicken in ranch dressing; shake off excess. Transfer chicken to panko; toss to coat, pressing panko into chicken. Place on prepared baking sheets.

3. Spray with cooking spray. Bake 15 to 17 minutes or until golden brown and cooked through, turning once.

herb cheese twists

Makes 10 twists

2 tablespoons butter
¼ cup grated Parmesan cheese
1 teaspoon dried parsley flakes
1 teaspoon dried basil
1 can (about 6 ounces) refrigerated buttermilk biscuits (5 count)

1. Preheat oven to 400°F. Grease baking sheet. Microwave butter in small microwavable bowl on MEDIUM (50%) just until melted; cool slightly. Stir in cheese, parsley and basil.

2. Pat each biscuit into 5×2-inch rectangle. Spread 1 teaspoon butter mixture onto each rectangle; cut each in half lengthwise. Twist each strip 3 or 4 times. Place on prepared baking sheet. Bake 8 minutes or until golden brown.

mini reuben skewers with dipping sauce

mini reuben skewers with dipping sauce

Makes 40 servings

⅓ cup HELLMANN'S® or BEST FOODS® Real Mayonnaise
⅓ cup WISH-BONE® Thousand Island Dressing
1 can (8 ounces) sauerkraut, drained and coarsely chopped
4 thin slices rye bread, crust removed
8 ounces sliced Swiss cheese
8 ounces sliced cooked corned beef or pastrami

1. Combine HELLMANN'S® or BEST FOODS® Real Mayonnaise, WISH-BONE® Thousand Island Dressing and sauerkraut in medium bowl; set aside.

2. Top 2 bread slices evenly with cheese, corned beef, then remaining bread. Cut each sandwich into 20 cubes and secure with wooden toothpicks. Serve with dipping sauce.

Prep Time: 10 minutes

bacon-wrapped fingerling potatoes with thyme

Makes 4 to 6 servings

1 pound fingerling potatoes
2 tablespoons olive oil
1 tablespoon minced fresh thyme
½ teaspoon black pepper
¼ teaspoon paprika
½ pound bacon strips
¼ cup chicken broth

Slow Cooker Directions

1. Toss potatoes with oil, thyme, pepper and paprika in large bowl.

2. Cut each bacon slice in half lengthwise; wrap half slice bacon tightly around each potato.

3. Heat large skillet over medium heat; add potatoes. Reduce heat to medium-low; cook until lightly browned and bacon has tightened around potatoes.

4. Place potatoes in **CROCK-POT®** slow cooker. Add broth. Cover; cook on HIGH 3 hours.

Prep Time: 45 minutes
Cook Time: 3 hours

cheddar nacho dip

Makes 2¾ cups

1 jar (1 pound) RAGÚ® Cheesy!®
   Double Cheddar Sauce
¾ cup prepared salsa

1. In 1-quart saucepan, heat Double Cheddar Sauce with salsa over medium heat, stirring occasionally.

2. Serve, if desired, with tortilla chips.

Prep Time: 5 minutes
Cook Time: 5 minutes

walnut-granola clusters

Makes about 5 dozen clusters

¼ cup (½ stick) butter
1 (10½-ounce) package miniature
   marshmallows
½ teaspoon ground cinnamon
3 cups rolled oats
2 cups chopped California walnuts
1 cup flaked coconut
2 (1-ounce) squares semi-sweet
   chocolate

Microwave butter in large microwavable mixing bowl at HIGH (100% power) 40 seconds or until melted. Stir in marshmallows and cinnamon. Microwave 1½ minutes or until melted, stirring halfway through cooking time. Quickly stir in oats, walnuts and coconut. With wet hands, form mixture into small balls and place on wax paper-lined baking sheets.

Microwave chocolate in glass measuring cup at HIGH 2½ minutes or until melted; stir. Lightly drizzle chocolate over clusters. Clusters may be stored at room temperature, covered, 4 to 5 days.

Favorite recipe from **Walnut Marketing Board**

Tip: Serve these tasty Walnut-Granola Clusters as an after-school snack or pack them in a sandwich bag to take along with you on road trips and other adventures.

bacon-wrapped fingerling potatoes with thyme

mexican drumsticks with ranchero dipping sauce

Makes 12 appetizers

12 chicken drumsticks
(about 3 pounds)
1 packet (1.25 ounces) ORTEGA®
Taco Seasoning Mix
1 bottle (8 ounces) ORTEGA®
Taco Sauce
1 bottle (8 ounces) ranch dressing
1 cup ORTEGA® Original Salsa

PREHEAT oven to 350°F. Arrange drumsticks on baking pan. Sprinkle seasoning mix over drumsticks, turning to coat both sides.

BAKE 45 minutes; turn drumsticks over halfway through to bake evenly. Remove from oven.

PLACE taco sauce in large mixing bowl. Add drumsticks and toss to coat evenly. Replace on baking sheet; broil 4 minutes on each side or until crisp.

COMBINE ranch dressing and salsa to make dipping sauce; mix well. Serve with warm drumsticks.

Prep Time: 5 minutes
Start-to-Finish Time: 1 hour

Tip: Always be prepared for company by keeping your pantry stocked with the ingredients to make these tangy drumsticks and creamy dip.

kicking cajun popcorn mix

Makes about 12 cups

1 bag popped JOLLY TIME®
Blast O Butter Microwave
Pop Corn (about 10 to 12 cups)
½ teaspoon Cajun seasoning
1 package (1.75 ounces) spicy
seasoned peanuts (⅓ cup)
1 tablespoon green pepper sauce
(optional)
2 cups hot & spicy cheese crackers
or jalapeño-flavored pretzel
nuggets

1. Preheat oven to 250°F.

2. Pop popcorn according to package directions. Open bag carefully; add seasoning and peanuts. Hold top of bag tightly and shake vigorously until seasoning is evenly distributed over popcorn.

3. Evenly spread popcorn mixture on large baking sheet; remove any unpopped kernels. Drizzle with optional green pepper sauce; stir. Bake 10 to 15 minutes; stir once during baking.

4. Toss in crackers or pretzel nuggets. Store at room temperature in airtight container.

mexican drumsticks with ranchero dipping sauce

cheesy potato skins

Makes 16 servings

4 large baked potatoes
2 tablespoons butter or margarine, melted
¼ pound (4 ounces) **VELVEETA®** Pasteurized Prepared Cheese Product, cut into ½-inch cubes
2 tablespoons chopped red bell peppers
2 slices **OSCAR MAYER®** Bacon, crisply cooked, crumbled
1 tablespoon sliced green onions

PREHEAT oven to 450°F. Cut potatoes in half lengthwise; scoop out centers, leaving ¼-inch-thick shells. (Refrigerate removed potato centers for another use.) Cut shells crosswise in half. Place, skin-sides down, on baking sheet; brush with butter.

BAKE 20 to 25 minutes or until crisp and golden brown.

FILL shells evenly with VELVEETA®; continue baking until VELVEETA® begins to melt. Top with remaining ingredients.

Prep Time: 15 minutes
Total Time: 35 minutes

cheesy potato skins

indian-spiced walnuts

Makes 4 cups

2 egg whites, lightly beaten
1 tablespoon ground cumin
1½ teaspoons curry powder
1½ teaspoons salt
½ teaspoon sugar
4 cups California walnuts, halves and pieces

Preheat oven to 350°F. Coat large, shallow baking pan with nonstick cooking spray. In large bowl, mix egg whites with spices, salt and sugar. Stir in walnuts and coat thoroughly. Spread in prepared pan. Bake 15 to 18 minutes or until dry and crisp. Cool completely before serving.

Favorite recipe from **Walnut Marketing Board**

black bean cakes

Makes 4 servings

1 can (about 15 ounces) black beans, rinsed and drained
¼ cup all-purpose flour
¼ cup chopped fresh cilantro
2 tablespoons plain yogurt or sour cream
1 tablespoon chili powder
2 cloves garlic, minced
1 tablespoon oil
Salsa

1. Place beans in medium bowl; mash with fork or potato masher until almost smooth, leaving some beans in larger pieces. Stir in flour, cilantro, yogurt, chili powder and garlic. Shape bean mixture into 8 patties.

2. Heat oil in large nonstick skillet over medium-high heat. Cook patties 6 to 8 minutes or until lightly browned, turning once. Serve with salsa.

hush puppies

hush puppies

Makes 12 hush puppies

Vegetable oil for frying
1 cup CREAM OF WHEAT® Hot
    Cereal (Instant, 1-minute,
    2½-minute or 10-minute
    cook time), uncooked
⅓ cup milk
1 egg
¼ cup minced onions
1 tablespoon honey
½ teaspoon salt

1. Preheat oil in deep fryer or heavy saucepan to 360°F. Combine remaining ingredients in medium bowl. Let stand 5 minutes.

2. Using two tablespoons, form batter into 1-inch balls and drop into hot oil. Cook 3 minutes or until brown and crispy. Remove with slotted spoon and drain on paper towels. Serve warm.

Prep Time: 10 minutes
Start-to-Finish Time: 15 minutes

Tip: Hush puppies are so delicious that they need no accompaniment, but they can be served with butter for spreading or a dipping sauce, such as tartar sauce or cocktail sauce.

buffalo wedges

3 pounds unpeeled Yukon Gold
  potatoes
3 tablespoons hot pepper sauce
2 tablespoons butter, melted
2 teaspoons smoked or sweet
  paprika
Blue cheese dressing

1. Preheat oven to 400°F. Spray baking
sheet with nonstick cooking spray.
Slice each potato into 4 to 6 wedges,
depending on size of potato.

2. Combine hot pepper sauce, butter
and paprika in large bowl. Add potato
wedges; toss to coat well. Place wedges
in single layer on prepared baking sheet.

3. Bake 20 minutes. Turn; bake
20 minutes or until light golden brown
and crisp. Serve with blue cheese
dressing.

bacon & onion dip

1 package (8 ounces)
  PHILADELPHIA® Cream Cheese,
  softened
3 tablespoons milk
6 slices OSCAR MAYER® Bacon,
  crisply cooked, crumbled
2 tablespoons sliced green onion
1 teaspoon KRAFT® Prepared
  Horseradish

BEAT cream cheese and milk with
electric mixer on medium speed until
well blended.

ADD remaining ingredients; mix well.
Cover. Refrigerate several hours or until
chilled. Serve with assorted NABISCO®
Crackers, cut-up vegetables, STELLA
D'ORO® Breadsticks or chips.

four cheese spread

1 package (8 ounces) cream cheese,
  softened
1 cup shredded Swiss cheese
  (about 4 ounces)
1 cup shredded fontina or Monterey
  Jack cheese (about 4 ounces)
½ cup sour cream
¼ cup grated Parmesan cheese
¼ cup finely chopped fresh basil
  leaves *or* 1½ teaspoons dried
  basil leaves, crushed
1 tablespoon finely chopped fresh
  parsley
1 tablespoon lemon juice
1 envelope LIPTON® RECIPE
  SECRETS® Vegetable Soup Mix

1. Line 4-cup mold or bowl with waxed
paper or dampened cheese cloth; set
aside.

2. With food processor or electric mixer,
combine all ingredients until smooth.
Pack into prepared mold; cover and
chill.

3. To serve, unmold onto serving platter
and remove waxed paper. Garnish,
if desired, with additional chopped
parsley and basil. Serve, if desired,
with assorted crackers, bagel chips or
cucumber slices.

Tip: Using a variety of cheeses gives
this spread a more complex and
nuanced flavor than recipes with only
one or two types.

summer salad lettuce wraps

Makes 3 servings

¼ cup extra virgin olive oil
  Juice from 1 lime
1 tablespoon red wine vinegar
1 cup grape tomatoes, halved
1 cup corn
½ cup diced fresh mozzarella cheese
¼ cup diced red onion
¼ cup chopped fresh basil
  Salt and black pepper
6 crunchy lettuce leaves

1. Whisk oil, lime juice and vinegar in large bowl.

2. Add tomatoes, corn, cheese, onion and basil; toss to coat. Season with salt and pepper.

3. To serve, scoop ¼ cup salad mixture onto each lettuce leaf. Fold to eat.

prosciutto-wrapped white nectarines

Makes 20 servings

2 large fresh California
  SUMMERWHITE® nectarines
20 thin strips prosciutto (about
  4 ounces total)
½ cup crumbled Gorgonzola cheese

Preheat broiler and line a baking sheet with foil. Cut each nectarine into 10 slices and wrap each with a prosciutto strip. Place on prepared baking sheet and broil for 2 to 3 minutes on each side or until prosciutto is crispy. While warm, sprinkle with cheese. Serve with toothpicks.

Favorite recipe from **California Tree Fruit Agreement**

clams posilippo

Makes 6 servings

2 dozen cherrystone clams, well
  scrubbed
½ cup finely chopped red or yellow
  bell pepper
½ cup finely chopped plum tomatoes
½ cup finely chopped green onions
¼ cup chopped Canadian bacon or
  boiled ham
¼ cup *Frank's® RedHot®* Original
  Cayenne Pepper Sauce
2 tablespoons olive oil
2 tablespoons grated Parmesan
  cheese

1. Place clams in large nonstick skillet; add ¼ cup water. Cook, covered, over medium heat 6 to 8 minutes or until clams begin to open, removing them to dish as they open. Rinse clams under water to remove excess sand, if necessary. Remove top shells; discard. With paring knife, loosen clam meat from bottom shell. Place clams in shallow ovenproof baking dish.

2. Preheat oven to 400°F. Combine bell pepper, tomatoes, onions, bacon, *Frank's RedHot* Sauce and oil in small bowl. Spoon about 1 tablespoon mixture over each clam. Sprinkle with cheese.

3. Bake clams 10 minutes or until heated through.

Prep Time: 25 minutes
Cook Time: 10 minutes

curried snack mix

curried snack mix

Makes 16 servings

3 tablespoons butter
2 tablespoons packed light brown sugar
1½ teaspoons hot curry powder
¼ teaspoon salt
¼ teaspoon ground cumin
2 cups rice cereal squares
1 cup walnut halves
1 cup dried cranberries

Slow Cooker Directions
Melt butter in large skillet. Add brown sugar, curry powder, salt and cumin; mix well. Add cereal, walnuts and cranberries; stir to coat. Transfer mixture to **CROCK-POT®** slow cooker. Cover; cook on LOW 3 hours. Uncover; cook 30 minutes.

Prep Time: 5 minutes
Cook Time: 3½ hours

tangy baked wings

Makes 12 servings

1 envelope (about 1 ounce) dry
   onion soup and recipe mix
⅓ cup honey
2 tablespoons spicy brown mustard
18 chicken wings (about 3 pounds)

1. Stir the soup mix, honey and mustard in a large bowl.

2. Cut off the chicken wing ends and discard. Cut the chicken wings in half at the joint. Add the chicken to the soup mixture and toss to coat. Place the chicken into a large shallow-sided baking pan.

3. Bake at 400°F. for 45 minutes or until the chicken is cooked through, turning over once halfway through cooking time.

southwestern popcorn shrimp dip

Makes 8 servings

1 carton (20 ounces) SEAPAK®
   Popcorn Shrimp
1 cup mayonnaise
1 chipotle pepper in adobo sauce,
   minced (about 1 tablespoon)
2 cups frozen corn, thawed
1 large red pepper, diced
1 bunch of green onions, thinly sliced
   Crackers or crostinis

Prepare the shrimp according to package directions. Roughly chop shrimp and set aside.

Stir mayonnaise and chipotle pepper in adobo sauce in large bowl. Add the chopped cooked shrimp, corn, red pepper and green onions. Toss to coat.

Scoop shrimp mixture into a serving bowl and serve with crackers or crostinis.

poblano pepper kabobs

Makes 4 servings

1 large poblano pepper
4 ounces smoked turkey breast, cut
   into 8 cubes
4 ounces pepper jack cheese, cut
   into 8 cubes
¼ cup salsa (optional)

1. Preheat oven to 400°F. Fill medium saucepan half full with water; bring to a boil over medium-high heat. Add poblano pepper; cook 1 minute. Drain. Core, seed and cut pepper into 12 bite-size pieces.

2. Thread 1 piece pepper, 1 piece turkey and 1 piece cheese onto each of 4 skewers. Repeat, ending with pepper.

3. Place kabobs on baking sheet. Bake 3 minutes or until cheese starts to melt. Serve with salsa, if desired.

tangy baked wings

sausage and pineapple quesadillas

Makes 8 servings

1 package HILLSHIRE FARM®
  Smoked Sausage
8 large (10-inch) flour tortillas
1 package (16 ounces) shredded
  Mexican cheese blend
1 can (20 ounces) pineapple tidbits,
  drained
½ cup sliced green onions
½ cup sliced pitted ripe black olives
  Salsa, sour cream and chopped
  fresh cilantro (optional)

1. Cut sausage into ¼-inch slices. Heat a large nonstick skillet over medium-high heat for 3 minutes. Add sausage and cook, stirring frequently, 3 to 4 minutes or until lightly browned. Remove sausage and drippings from pan.

2. Reduce heat to medium. Place one tortilla in pan. Top with ¼ each of cheese, sausage, pineapple, green onions and black olives. Place another tortilla on top.

3. Cook quesadilla for 1 to 2 minutes or until bottom is crisp and lightly browned. Carefully flip quesadilla and cook second side 1 to 2 minutes or until lightly browned and cheese is melted. Remove quesadilla from pan and repeat with remaining ingredients.

4. Cut each quesadilla into 8 wedges and serve with salsa, sour cream and chopped cilantro, if desired.

hot artichoke dip

Makes 3¼ cups

1 package (8 ounces)
  PHILADELPHIA® Cream Cheese,
  softened
1 can (14 ounces) artichoke hearts,
  drained, chopped
½ cup KRAFT® Mayo Real
  Mayonnaise
½ cup KRAFT® 100% Grated
  Parmesan Cheese
2 tablespoons finely chopped fresh
  basil or 1 teaspoon dried basil
  leaves
2 tablespoons finely chopped red
  onion
1 clove garlic, minced
½ cup chopped tomato

BEAT cream cheese and all remaining ingredients except tomato with electric mixer on medium speed until well blended.

SPOON into 9-inch pie plate.

BAKE at 350°F for 25 minutes. Sprinkle with tomato. Serve with assorted cut-up vegetables, NABISCO® Crackers or Baked Pita Bread Wedges.

Baked Pita Bread Wedges: Cut each of 3 split pita breads into 8 triangles. Place on cookie sheet. Bake at 350°F for 10 to 12 minutes or until crisp.

Prep Time: 15 minutes
Bake Time: 25 minutes

easy cheesy artichoke & spinach bread

Makes 8 servings

1 can (14 ounces) artichoke hearts, drained and chopped
1 package (10 ounces) frozen chopped spinach, thawed and squeezed dry
1 cup HELLMANN'S® or BEST FOODS® Real Mayonnaise
1 cup grated Parmesan cheese
1 clove garlic, finely chopped
1 loaf French or Italian bread (about 16 inches long), halved lengthwise

1. Preheat oven to 350°F.

2. In small bowl, combine all ingredients except bread; evenly spread on bread. Bake 12 minutes or until golden and heated through.

Prep Time: 10 minutes
Cook Time: 12 minutes

easy cheesy artichoke & spinach bread

double onion crunchy rings

Makes about 2½ dozen pieces

2 cups *French's®* French Fried Onions
¼ cup plus 2 tablespoons all-purpose flour, divided
2 cups medium onions, cut into ½-inch rings
2 egg whites, beaten

1. Heat oven to 400°F. Place French Fried Onions and *2 tablespoons* flour into plastic bag. Lightly crush with hands or with rolling pin. Place *¼ cup* flour into separate plastic bag. Toss onion rings in ¼ cup flour; shake off excess.

2. Dip floured onion rings into beaten egg whites. Coat in crushed onions, pressing firmly to adhere.

3. Place rings on lightly greased baking rack set over rimmed baking sheet. Bake 10 minutes or until onions are tender.

Prep Time: 15 minutes
Cook Time: 10 minutes

bacon orange marmalade spread

Makes about 2½ cups

2 packages (8 ounces each) reduced-fat cream cheese, softened
6 slices well-cooked bacon, blotted, then crumbled
2 green onions, thinly sliced
¼ cup POLANER® Sugar Free Orange Marmalade with Fiber

BEAT cream cheese in a medium bowl with an electric mixer until smooth.

STIR in remaining ingredients until thoroughly combined. Refrigerate.

fruit kabobs with raspberry yogurt dip

Makes 6 servings

½ cup plain yogurt
¼ cup raspberry fruit spread
1 pint strawberries
2 cups cubed honeydew melon
(1-inch cubes)
2 cups cubed cantaloupe
(1-inch cubes)
1 can (8 ounces) pineapple chunks
in juice, drained

1. Combine yogurt and fruit spread in small bowl until well blended.

2. Thread fruit onto six 12-inch wooden skewers. Serve with dip.

fruit kabobs with raspberry yogurt dip

cucumber roulades

Makes 6 servings

1 seedless cucumber, peeled
¼ cup PHILADELPHIA® Chive &
Onion Cream Cheese Spread
1 ounce smoked salmon, thinly
sliced, cut into 12 pieces
12 sprigs fresh dill

CUT cucumber crosswise into 12 slices. Use a melon baller to scoop out indentation in center of each cucumber round.

FILL evenly with cream cheese spread. Top with salmon and dill.

Tip: Smoked salmon is simply that—salmon that has been smoked, either at "cold" or "hot" temperatures—while traditional lox has gone through the additional step of being cured in a salt-sugar solution.

smoked turkey roll-ups

Makes 56 pieces

2 packages (4 ounces each)
herb-flavored soft spreadable
cheese, at room temperature
4 (8-inch) flour tortillas
12 ounces smoked turkey breast slices
2 green onions, minced
¼ cup roasted red peppers, drained
and finely chopped

1. Spread one package of cheese evenly over tortillas. Layer 3 ounces turkey slices evenly over cheese, overlapping turkey slices slightly to cover each tortilla. Spread remaining package of cheese evenly over turkey slices. Sprinkle with green onions and red peppers.

2. Tightly roll up each tortilla jelly-roll style. Place roll-ups, seam side down, in resealable plastic bag; refrigerate several hours or overnight.

3. To serve, trim edges and cut each roll-up crosswise into ½-inch slices to form pinwheels. If desired, arrange pinwheels on serving plate and garnish with red pepper slices in center.

Favorite recipe from **National Turkey Federation**

crispy bacon sticks

Makes 10 sticks

½ cup (1½ ounces) grated Wisconsin
  Parmesan cheese, divided
5 slices bacon, halved lengthwise
10 breadsticks

Microwave Directions
Spread ¼ cup cheese on plate. Press
one side of bacon into cheese; wrap
diagonally around breadstick with
cheese-coated side toward stick. Place
on paper plate or microwave-safe baking
sheet lined with paper towels. Repeat
with remaining bacon halves, cheese
and breadsticks. Microwave on HIGH
4 to 6 minutes or until bacon is cooked,
checking for doneness after 4 minutes.
Roll again in remaining ¼ cup Parmesan
cheese. Serve warm.

Favorite recipe from **Wisconsin Milk
Marketing Board**

spinach & chèvre dip

Makes 2 cups dip

1 package (10 ounces) frozen
  chopped spinach, thawed and
  squeezed dry
1 cup plain nonfat yogurt
½ cup (2 ounces) crumbled goat
  cheese
¼ cup *French's*® Honey Dijon Mustard
2 tablespoons chopped fresh basil
1 clove garlic, chopped
¼ teaspoon black pepper

1. Place spinach, yogurt, cheese,
mustard, basil, garlic and pepper in food
processor or blender. Cover and process
until well blended but slightly chunky.
Cover and refrigerate 1 hour before
serving.

2. Serve with vegetable crudités or
crackers, if desired.

polenta triangles

Makes about 24 triangles

3 cups cold water
1 cup yellow cornmeal
1 envelope LIPTON® RECIPE
  SECRETS® Golden Onion or
  Onion Soup Mix
1 can (4 ounces) mild chopped green
  chiles, drained
½ cup thawed frozen or drained
  canned whole kernel corn
⅓ cup finely chopped roasted red
  peppers
½ cup shredded sharp Cheddar
  cheese (about 2 ounces)

1. In 3-quart saucepan, bring water to
a boil over high heat. With wire whisk,
stir in cornmeal, then soup mix. Reduce
heat to low and simmer uncovered,
stirring constantly, 25 minutes or until
thickened. Stir in chiles, corn and
roasted red peppers.

2. Spread into lightly greased 9-inch
square baking pan; sprinkle with
cheese. Let stand 20 minutes or until
firm; cut into triangles. Serve at room
temperature or heat in oven at 350°F
for 5 minutes or until warm.

Tip: To roast bell peppers, preheat
the broiler. Broil peppers on a foil-
covered broiler pan 4 inches from
heat 15 to 20 minutes until blackened
on all sides, turning every 5 minutes.
Transfer to medium bowl; cover with
plastic wrap. Let stand 15 minutes.
Core peppers and remove and discard
skin. Place any leftovers in an airtight
container, cover with olive oil, and
refrigerate for up to 1 week.

crispy bacon sticks

stromboli sticks

Makes 10 sticks

- 1 package (13.8 ounces) refrigerated pizza crust dough
- 10 mozzarella cheese sticks
- 30 thin slices pepperoni
- 1 jar (1 pound 10 ounces) RAGÚ® Old World Style® Pasta Sauce, heated

1. Preheat oven to 425°F. Grease baking sheet; set aside.

2. Roll pizza dough into 13×10-inch rectangle. Cut in half crosswise, then cut each half into 5 strips.

3. Arrange 1 cheese stick on each strip of pizza dough, then top with 3 slices pepperoni. Fold edges over, sealing tightly.

4. Arrange stromboli sticks on prepared baking sheet, seam side down. Bake 15 minutes or until golden. Serve with Pasta Sauce for dipping.

Prep Time: 15 minutes
Cook Time: 15 minutes

piña colada brie

Makes 6 servings

- 1 wheel (1 pound) Brie cheese
- 1 can (8 ounces) DOLE® Crushed Pineapple, drained
- 3 tablespoons honey-roasted peanuts or sliced almonds
- 2 tablespoons brown sugar
- 2 tablespoons flaked coconut
  French bread or crackers

• Place cheese on ovenproof serving platter. Combine drained crushed pineapple, peanuts and sugar in small saucepan. Cook until thoroughly heated. Spoon mixture over cheese.

• Bake at 400°F. 8 to 10 minutes or until cheese is softened. Sprinkle coconut over pineapple topping; continue to bake just until coconut is lightly toasted.

• Serve with French bread or crackers.

Prep Time: 5 minutes
Cook Time: 15 minutes

orange maple sausage balls

Makes about 24 appetizers

- 1 pound BOB EVANS® Original Recipe Roll Sausage
- 1 small onion, finely chopped
- 1 small red or yellow bell pepper, finely chopped
- 1 egg
- 2 tablespoons uncooked cream of wheat cereal
- ½ cup maple syrup or maple-flavored syrup
- 3 to 5 tablespoons frozen orange juice concentrate, slightly thawed, to taste

Combine first 5 ingredients in large bowl until well blended. Shape into ¾-inch balls. Cook in large skillet over medium-high heat until browned on all sides and no longer pink in centers. Drain off drippings. Add syrup and orange juice concentrate to sausage mixture. Cook and stir over medium heat 2 to 3 minutes or until thick bubbly syrup forms. Serve hot. Refrigerate leftovers.

picnic pizza muffins

picnic pizza muffins

Makes 8 servings

1 package (about 1 pound)
    refrigerated grand-size flaky
    buttermilk biscuits
1 pound ground beef
½ cup chopped green bell pepper
½ cup canned sliced mushrooms,
    drained
½ cup pizza sauce
½ cup shredded mozzarella cheese
2 tablespoons *Frank's® RedHot®*
    Original Cayenne Pepper Sauce

1. Preheat oven to 375°F. Separate
biscuits; pat into 3-inch circles. Press
circles into muffin cups. Fill empty
muffin cups halfway with water. Set
aside.

2. Cook beef and vegetables in large
nonstick skillet over high heat 5 to
8 minutes or until meat is browned,
stirring to separate meat. Drain fat.
Stir in pizza sauce, cheese and *Frank's
RedHot* Sauce; mix well.

3. Mound filling into muffin cups,
dividing evenly. Bake 20 minutes or
until muffins are browned. Serve warm
or at room temperature.

Prep Time: 15 minutes
Cook Time: 25 minutes

lamb meatballs with tomato mint dip

Makes 10 dozen meatballs

1½ cups fine bulgur wheat
3 cups cold water
2 pounds ground AMERICAN LAMB
1 cup minced fresh parsley
2 medium onions, minced
1 tablespoon salt
½ teaspoon ground allspice
½ teaspoon ground cinnamon
½ teaspoon ground nutmeg
½ teaspoon black pepper
¼ to ½ teaspoon ground red pepper
1 piece fresh ginger, about 2×1-inch,
    peeled and minced
    Tomato Mint Dip (recipe follows)

Place bulgur in medium bowl: add
water. Let soak about 10 minutes. Drain
and place in fine meshed strainer;
squeeze out water.

In large bowl, knead lamb with parsley,
onions, seasonings and ginger. Add
bulgur; knead well. Add enough ice
water to keep mixture smooth (up to
1 cup). Use about 1 teaspoon meat
mixture to make bite-sized meatballs.
Place on ungreased jelly-roll pan. Bake
in preheated 375°F oven 20 minutes.
Meanwhile, prepare Tomato Mint Dip.

Place meatballs in serving bowl; keep
warm. Serve hot with dip.

tomato mint dip

2 cans (15 ounces each) tomato
    sauce with tomato bits
1½ teaspoons ground allspice
1 teaspoon dried mint

In small saucepan, heat all ingredients
about 5 minutes to blend flavors.

Favorite recipe from **American Lamb
Board**

cajun deviled eggs

Makes 6 servings

- 6 hard-cooked eggs, peeled
- 3 tablespoons mayonnaise
- ½ teaspoon Cajun or Creole seasoning, divided
- 2 tablespoons chopped fresh parsley

1. Slice eggs in half lengthwise. Place yolks in small bowl. Add mayonnaise and seasoning; mix well. Pipe or spoon filling into egg whites.

2. Cover and chill at least 30 minutes or up to 24 hours before serving. Sprinkle with parsley just before serving.

tangy wisconsin blue cheese whip

Makes about 2 cups

- 1 cup whipping cream
- ½ cup finely crumbled Wisconsin Blue cheese (2 ounces)
- 1 teaspoon dried basil, crushed
- ¼ teaspoon garlic salt
- ½ cup almonds, toasted and chopped Assorted vegetable or fruit dippers

In a small mixer bowl, combine whipping cream, Blue cheese, basil and garlic salt. Beat with an electric mixer on medium speed until slightly thickened. Gently fold in chopped almonds. Serve with vegetable or fruit dippers. (Dip can be made ahead and chilled, covered, up to 2 hours.)

Favorite recipe from **Wisconsin Milk Marketing Board**

mini new potato bites

Makes 15 servings

- 1½ pounds new potatoes (about 15 potatoes)
- 4 ounces (½ of 8-ounce package) PHILADELPHIA® Cream Cheese, softened
- 2 tablespoons BREAKSTONE'S® or KNUDSEN® Sour Cream
- 2 tablespoons KRAFT® 100% Grated Parmesan Cheese
- 4 slices OSCAR MAYER® Bacon, cooked, crumbled
- 2 tablespoons snipped fresh chives

PLACE potatoes in large saucepan; add enough water to cover. Bring to boil. Reduce heat to medium-low; cook 15 minutes or until potatoes are tender.

MIX cream cheese, sour cream and Parmesan cheese in small bowl; cover. Refrigerate until ready to use.

DRAIN potatoes. Cool slightly. Cut potatoes in half; cut small piece from bottom of each potato half so potato lies flat. Place on serving platter. Top each potato half with 1 teaspoon of the cream cheese mixture. Sprinkle with bacon and chives.

mini new potato bites

cocktail wraps

Makes 8 servings

**16 HILLSHIRE FARM® Lit'l Smokies®
Cocktail Links
16 thin strips Cheddar, Swiss or hot
pepper cheese
1 package (8 ounces) refrigerated
crescent roll dough
Mustard (optional)**

1. Preheat oven to 400°F. Cut a thin slit in each sausage. Place 1 cheese strip inside slit of each sausage.

2. Separate crescent roll dough into 8 triangles. Cut each triangle in half lengthwise to form 2 smaller triangles. Place 1 sausage on wide end of triangle and roll towards the point. Place wrapped sausage, point side down, on baking sheet. Repeat with remaining sausages.

3. Bake 9 to 10 minutes or until golden brown. Serve with mustard, if desired.

arugula canapes

Makes 6 dozen canapes

**3 tablespoons mayonnaise
1 teaspoon lemon juice
¼ teaspoon Original TABASCO®
brand Pepper Sauce
¼ teaspoon salt
1 cup finely chopped arugula
½ cup finely chopped watercress
1 whole green onion, finely chopped
Thinly sliced white bread
Softened butter**

Mix mayonnaise, lemon juice, TABASCO® Sauce and salt in small bowl. Stir in arugula, watercress and green onion; mix well.

Cut 1½-inch rounds from bread; spread lightly with butter. Spread ½ teaspoon arugula mixture on each bread round. Cover with plastic wrap and chill until ready to serve.

honey caramel popcorn

Makes 12 cups

**12 cups popped popcorn
3 cups mixed nuts
½ cup granulated sugar
½ cup packed brown sugar
½ cup honey or light corn syrup
½ cup (1 stick) butter
1 teaspoon cinnamon
½ teaspoon salt
1 teaspoon baking soda
1 teaspoon vanilla**

1. Preheat oven to 250°F. Spray large shallow baking pan with nonstick cooking spray. Combine popcorn and nuts in large bowl.

2. Combine granulated sugar, brown sugar, honey, butter, cinnamon and salt in large saucepan. Bring to a boil over medium heat, stirring constantly. Boil 5 minutes. *Do not stir.* Remove from heat; stir in baking soda and vanilla. Pour over popcorn mixture, stirring to coat. Spread mixture on prepared pan.

3. Bake 45 minutes, stirring occasionally. Remove to wire rack; cool completely. Break apart; store in tightly covered container.

heavenly ham roll-ups

heavenly ham roll-ups

Makes 15 servings

1 package (9 ounces)
    OSCAR MAYER® Shaved
    Smoked Ham
5 tablespoons PHILADELPHIA® Light
    Cream Cheese Spread
15 asparagus spears (about 1 pound),
    trimmed

PREHEAT oven to 350°F. Flatten ham slices; pat dry. Stack ham in piles of 2 slices each; spread each stack with 1 teaspoon of the cream cheese spread.

PLACE 1 asparagus spear on one of the long sides of each ham stack; roll up. Place in 13×9-inch baking dish.

BAKE 15 to 20 minutes or until heated through.

Prep Time: 15 minutes
Bake Time: 20 minutes

pecan cheese ball

Makes 1 cheese ball

2 packages (8 ounces each) cream
    cheese, softened
1 package (8 ounces) shredded
    Cheddar cheese
1 envelope LIPTON® RECIPE
    SECRETS® Onion Soup Mix
2 tablespoons finely chopped fresh
    parsley
½ teaspoon garlic powder
½ cup finely chopped pecans,
    toasted, if desired

1. In large bowl, with electric mixer, beat cream cheese until light and fluffy, about 2 minutes. Stir in Cheddar cheese, soup mix, parsley and garlic powder.

2. Wet hands with cold water. Shape cheese mixture into ball. Roll cheese ball in pecans until evenly coated.

3. Refrigerate 1 hour or until set. Serve with crackers.

Prep Time: 15 minutes
Chill Time: 1 hour

peanut butter granola balls

Makes 4 servings

½ cup SKIPPY® Creamy Peanut Butter
2 tablespoons honey
1 cup low-fat granola cereal
1 cup toasted rice cereal

In medium bowl, combine SKIPPY® Creamy Peanut Butter with honey. Stir in remaining ingredients. With slightly moistened hands, shape into 16 balls. Chill until ready to serve.

Prep Time: 15 minutes

soups
& salads

soups & salads

• • • • •

pepperoni pizza soup

Makes 4 servings

8 slices French baguette bread,
  ½-inch thick
1 tablespoon olive oil
2 tablespoons SARGENTO®
  ARTISAN BLENDS™ Shredded
  Parmesan Cheese
1 can (14½ ounces) chunky pasta-
  style stewed tomatoes
1 can (14½ ounces) chicken broth
2 cups sliced zucchini, ½-inch thick
1 large red bell pepper, cut into
  ¾-inch pieces
1 can (2¼ ounces) sliced black olives,
  drained
2 ounces thinly sliced pepperoni
1½ cups (6 ounces) SARGENTO®
  FANCY SHREDDED PIZZA
  DOUBLE CHEESE®
  Fresh basil sprigs (optional)

BRUSH bread slices with oil; sprinkle with Parmesan cheese. Place on baking sheet. Bake in preheated 400°F oven 6 minutes or until golden brown.

COMBINE tomatoes, chicken broth, zucchini and bell pepper in large saucepan. Heat to a boil; reduce heat. Simmer, uncovered, 5 minutes or until vegetables are crisp-tender. Stir in olives and pepperoni. Simmer 1 minute.

LADLE soup into 4 soup bowls; sprinkle evenly with Pizza Double Cheese. Top each serving with 2 bread slices. Garnish with basil sprigs, if desired.

Prep Time: 15 minutes
Cook Time: 12 minutes

margarita shrimp salad

Makes 4 servings

1 tablespoon lime juice
2 teaspoons grated lime zest
3 cloves garlic, minced
1 pound fresh large shrimp, peeled
   and deveined
¾ cup SWANSON® Chicken Stock
1 medium red **or** orange pepper,
   cut into 2-inch-long strips
   (about 1½ cups)
1 small onion, sliced (about ¼ cup)
¼ cup chopped fresh cilantro leaves
4 cups romaine lettuce **or** iceberg
   lettuce torn into bite-size pieces
2 large tomatoes, thickly sliced
¼ teaspoon ground black pepper

1. Stir the lime juice, lime zest and garlic in a 2-quart shallow nonmetallic baking dish or a gallon-size resealable plastic bag. Add the shrimp and toss to coat. Cover the dish or seal the bag and refrigerate for 30 minutes, turning the shrimp over several times during marinating.

2. Heat the stock in a 2-quart saucepan over medium-high heat to a boil. Add the red pepper and onion and cook until the vegetables are tender-crisp.

3. Reduce the heat to medium. Add the shrimp and marinade to the saucepan and cook until the shrimp are cooked through. Stir in the cilantro. Divide the lettuce, tomatoes and shrimp mixture among 4 serving plates. Sprinkle with the black pepper.

sopa de lima

Makes 6 servings

2 tablespoons olive oil
2 pounds chicken thighs and legs
1 cup chopped yellow onion
2 cloves garlic, minced
6 cups water
1 cup chopped tomatoes
1 jalapeño pepper,* minced
1 tablespoon chili powder
1 teaspoon ground cumin
1 teaspoon dried oregano
3 tablespoons lime juice
1 teaspoon salt
½ cup chopped fresh cilantro
¼ cup finely chopped radishes
   Lime wedges

Jalapeño peppers can sting and irritate the skin, so wear rubber gloves when handling peppers and do not touch your eyes.

1. Heat oil in Dutch oven over medium-high heat. Add chicken; brown on both sides. Transfer to plate.

2. Add onion and garlic to Dutch oven. Reduce heat to medium; cook and stir 3 minutes or until onion is translucent. Add water; bring to a boil. Add chicken, tomatoes, jalapeño pepper, chili powder, cumin and oregano. Reduce heat to low; cover and simmer 1 hour or until chicken is falling off bone. Remove chicken; cool slightly. Remove meat from bone, shred and return to Dutch oven. Stir in lime juice and salt.

3. Serve soup with cilantro, radishes and lime wedges.

clam chowder

clam chowder

Makes 5 servings

1 small onion, chopped
1 stalk celery, chopped
2 slices OSCAR MAYER® Bacon, chopped
1 pound potatoes, peeled, cut into ¼-inch cubes (about 2 cups)
1½ cups water
1 cup milk
4 ounces (½ of 8-ounce package) PHILADELPHIA® Cream Cheese, cubed
1 can (6¼ ounces) minced clams, undrained

COOK and stir onions, celery and bacon in medium saucepan on medium heat 5 minutes or until vegetables are crisp-tender.

ADD potatoes and water; bring to boil. Cook 15 minutes or until potatoes are tender.

MICROWAVE milk and cream cheese in small microwavable bowl on HIGH 1½ minutes or until milk is heated through. Stir with wire whisk until cream cheese is completely melted. Add to potato mixture; stir until well blended. Stir in the clams with their liquid. Cook 2 minutes or until heated through, stirring frequently. (Do not boil.)

spicy thai warm shrimp salad

Makes 6 servings

¾ cup prepared vinaigrette salad dressing
⅓ cup chopped fresh mint leaves
¼ cup *Frank's® RedHot®* XTRA Hot Sauce or *Frank's® RedHot®* Cayenne Pepper Sauce
¼ cup *French's®* Honey Dijon Mustard
1 tablespoon lime juice
1 tablespoon sucralose sugar substitute
1 tablespoon vegetable oil
1½ pounds large shrimp, shelled with tails left on
8 cups shredded Napa cabbage
1 red bell pepper, thinly sliced
1 cup thinly sliced cucumber

1. Combine salad dressing, mint, XTRA Hot Sauce, mustard, lime juice and sugar substitute in large bowl; set aside.

2. Heat oil in large nonstick skillet or wok until hot. Stir-fry shrimp 2 to 3 minutes until shrimp turn pink. Transfer to bowl with dressing. Add cabbage, bell pepper and cucumber; toss to coat. Serve warm.

Prep Time: 10 minutes
Cook Time: 5 minutes

Tip: Shrimp are grouped for retail purposes by their size. The most common sizes that you will find in your supermarket case are jumbo (11 to 15 per pound), large (21 to 30), medium (31 to 35) and small (36 to 45).

turkey club salad

Makes 4 servings

- 8 cups coarsely chopped romaine lettuce leaves
- 2 large hard-cooked eggs, diced
- 1 cup cherry tomatoes, halved
- 4 slices bacon, crisp-cooked and crumbled
- 1 package (4 ounces) blue cheese crumbles
- 8 slices deli turkey breast, rolled-up
- ½ cup WISH-BONE® Ranch Dressing

Arrange lettuce on large platter. Top with rows of eggs, tomatoes, bacon, cheese and turkey. Just before serving, drizzle with WISH-BONE® Ranch Dressing.

Prep Time: 15 minutes

black bean and rice salad

Makes 4 servings

- 1 cup MINUTE® White Rice, uncooked
- 1 can (15 ounces) black beans, drained, rinsed
- 1 medium red bell pepper, cut into thin strips
- ½ cup fat-free peppercorn ranch dressing
- 2 green onions, thinly sliced
- ¼ cup fresh cilantro, chopped
- 1 teaspoon ground cumin

Prepare rice according to package directions. Place in large bowl.

Add remaining ingredients; mix lightly. Cover.

Serve at room temperature or chill several hours before serving.

pumpkin and roasted pepper soup

Makes 6 servings

- 2 tablespoons butter
- 1 red onion, chopped
- 1 stalk celery, chopped
- 3 cups chicken broth
- 1 can (15 ounces) solid-pack pumpkin
- ½ cup chopped roasted red pepper
- ½ teaspoon salt
- ½ teaspoon paprika
- ¼ teaspoon dried thyme
- ¼ teaspoon black pepper
- 2 tablespoons half-and-half

1. Melt butter in large saucepan over medium-high heat. Add onion and celery; cook 5 minutes or until onion is translucent, stirring occasionally.

2. Add broth, pumpkin, roasted red pepper, salt, paprika, thyme and black pepper. Reduce heat to low; cook 30 minutes, stirring occasionally.

3. Working in batches, process soup in blender or food processor until smooth. Return soup to saucepan; stir in half-and-half. Cook until heated through, stirring occasionally.

turkey club salad

country chicken chowder

Makes 8 servings

2 tablespoons butter
1½ pounds chicken tenders, cut into
   ½-inch pieces
2 onions, chopped
2 stalks celery, sliced
2 carrots, sliced
2 cups frozen corn
2 cans (10¾ ounces each) condensed
   cream of potato soup, undiluted
1½ cups chicken broth
1 teaspoon dried dill weed
½ cup half-and-half

Slow Cooker Directions

1. Melt butter in large skillet over medium-high heat. Add chicken; cook and stir until browned.

2. Combine chicken, onions, celery, carrots, corn, soup, broth and dill weed in **CROCK-POT®** slow cooker. Cover; cook on LOW 3 to 4 hours or until vegetables are tender.

3. Turn off heat; stir in half-and-half. Cover; let stand 5 minutes or until heated through.

Note: For a special touch, garnish soup with croutons and fresh dill.

Tip: Chicken tenders, sometimes called "supremes," are the lean, tender strips that are found on the underside of the breast. They are skinless and boneless, so they require little prep work and cook quickly.

roasted pepper and avocado salad

Makes 6 servings

2 red bell peppers
2 orange bell peppers
2 yellow bell peppers
2 ripe avocados, halved, pitted and
   peeled
3 shallots, thinly sliced
¼ cup FILIPPO BERIO® Extra Virgin
   Olive Oil
1 clove garlic, crushed
   Finely grated peel and juice of
   1 lemon
   Salt and freshly ground black
   pepper

Place bell peppers on baking sheet. Broil, 4 to 5 inches from heat, 5 minutes on each side or until entire surface of each bell pepper is blistered and blackened slightly. Place bell peppers in paper bag. Close bag; cool 15 to 20 minutes.

Cut around cores of bell peppers; twist and remove. Cut bell peppers lengthwise in half. Peel off skin with paring knife; rinse under cold water to remove seeds. Slice bell peppers into ½-inch-thick strips; place in shallow dish.

Cut avocados into ¼-inch-thick slices; add to bell peppers. Sprinkle with shallots.

In small bowl, whisk together olive oil, garlic, lemon peel and juice. Pour over bell pepper mixture. Cover; refrigerate at least 1 hour before serving. Season to taste with salt and black pepper.

best-of-the-west bean salad

Makes 8 servings

- ¾ cup PACE® Picante Sauce
- 2 tablespoons chopped fresh cilantro leaves
- 2 tablespoons red wine vinegar
- 1 tablespoon vegetable oil
- 1 large green pepper, diced (about 1 cup)
- 1 medium red onion, very thinly sliced (about ½ cup)
- 1 can (about 15 ounces) kidney beans, rinsed and drained
- 1 can (about 15 ounces) pinto beans, rinsed and drained

Stir the picante sauce, cilantro, vinegar, oil, pepper, onion, kidney beans and pinto beans in a medium bowl. Cover and refrigerate for 2 hours, stirring occasionally during chilling time. Garnish with additional cilantro.

Prep Time: 10 minutes
Chill Time: 2 hours

fresh lime and black bean soup

Makes 4 servings

- 2 cans (about 15 ounces each) black beans, undrained
- 1 can (about 14 ounces) chicken broth
- 1½ cups chopped onions
- 1½ teaspoons chili powder
- ¾ teaspoon ground cumin
- ¼ teaspoon garlic powder
- ⅛ to ¼ teaspoon red pepper flakes
- ½ cup sour cream
- 2 tablespoons extra virgin olive oil
- 2 tablespoons chopped fresh cilantro
- 1 lime, cut into wedges

Slow Cooker Directions

1. Coat slow cooker with nonstick cooking spray. Add beans, broth, onions, chili powder, cumin, garlic powder and red pepper flakes. Cover; cook on LOW 7 hours or on HIGH 3½ hours.

2. To thicken soup, place half of soup mixture in food processor or blender. Process until smooth. Stir into remaining soup in slow cooker. Let stand 15 to 20 minutes before serving.

3. Serve soup with sour cream, oil, cilantro and lime wedges.

Prep Time: 10 minutes
Cook Time: 7 hours (LOW) or 3½ hours (HIGH)

chopped succotash salad

Makes 6 servings

- 8 cups chopped romaine lettuce leaves
- 1 pound cut-up cooked chicken
- 1 box (10 ounces) frozen lima beans, cooked, drained and rinsed with cold water
- 2 ears corn-on-the-cob, kernels removed (about 2 cups) or 2 cups frozen corn kernels, thawed
- 1 large red bell pepper, chopped
- ½ cup chopped red onion
- 2 slices bacon, crisp-cooked and crumbled
- 60 sprays WISH-BONE® SALAD SPRITZERS® Ranch Dressing

On large shallow serving platter, arrange lettuce. Evenly top with remaining ingredients, arranging in rows. Just before serving, spritz with WISH-BONE® SALAD SPRITZERS® Ranch Dressing.

Prep Time: 20 minutes

best-of-the-west bean salad

southwest grilled pork salad

southwest grilled pork salad

Makes 4 servings

½ cup mayonnaise
¼ cup orange juice
1 teaspoon grated orange peel
4 teaspoons chili powder
4 boneless pork chops
8 cups baby spinach leaves
2 oranges, cut into sections
1½ cups radishes, cut into matchsticks
1 cup *French's*® French Fried Onions

1. Mix mayonnaise, juice and peel; reserve. Rub chili powder onto both sides of pork.

2. Grill pork over medium-high heat until no longer pink in center; cut into cubes.

3. Arrange spinach, oranges, radishes and pork on serving plates.

4. Serve with dressing and top with French Fried Onions.

Prep Time: 10 minutes
Cook Time: 15 minutes

creamy asparagus soup with prosciutto

Makes 4 to 6 servings

1 tablespoon butter
1 large shallot, chopped
1 pound fresh asparagus spears, trimmed and cut into ½-inch pieces
2 cans (14½ ounces each) chicken broth
1 jar (15 ounces) CLASSICO® Creamy Alfredo Pasta Sauce
2 slices prosciutto, cut into thin strips and pan-fried*
1 cup garlic croutons (optional)

Lightly fry prosciutto strips in a dry skillet. For crispier prosciutto, fry in 1 tablespoon olive oil.

1. In medium saucepan, melt butter over medium heat. Add shallot; cook and stir 3 to 4 minutes.

2. Add asparagus and broth; bring to a boil. Reduce heat and simmer 10 to 15 minutes or until asparagus is tender. Remove from heat.

3. In food processor or blender, purée soup in batches until smooth. Return puréed soup to saucepan; stir in Alfredo sauce. Cook and stir over low heat until heated through. Season with salt and pepper, if desired. Serve hot, topped with prosciutto and croutons.

Tip: Prosciutto is a type of Italian ham. It is seasoned, cured and air-dried, not smoked. It is usually sold in very thin slices. Look for the imported Parma or less expensive domestic substitutes in delis and Italian food markets.

country turkey and veggie soup

country turkey and veggie soup

Makes 8 servings

2 tablespoons butter, divided
8 ounces sliced mushrooms
½ cup chopped onion
½ cup thinly sliced celery
1 red bell pepper, chopped
1 carrot, thinly sliced
½ teaspoon dried thyme
4 cups chicken or turkey broth
4 ounces uncooked egg noodles
2 cups chopped cooked turkey
1 cup half-and-half
½ cup frozen peas, thawed
  Salt and black pepper

Slow Cooker Directions

1. Melt 1 tablespoon butter in large nonstick skillet over medium-high heat. Add mushrooms and onion; cook and stir 4 minutes or until onion is translucent. Transfer to slow cooker.

2. Add celery, bell pepper, carrot and thyme to slow cooker; pour in broth. Cover; cook on HIGH 2½ hours.

3. Add noodles and turkey. Cover; cook 20 minutes. Stir in half-and half, peas and remaining 1 tablespoon butter. Season with salt and black pepper. Cook until noodles are tender and soup is heated through.

south asian curried potato salad

Makes 10 servings

2 pounds unpeeled new potatoes
1½ teaspoons salt, divided
¾ cup plain yogurt
½ cup diced onion
½ cup diced celery
⅓ cup diced green bell pepper
¼ cup mayonnaise
2 teaspoons curry powder
2 teaspoons lemon juice

1. Place potatoes and 1 teaspoon salt in large saucepan; add cold water to cover. Bring to a boil over high heat; boil 20 minutes or just until potatoes are tender. Drain; cool to room temperature.

2. Combine yogurt, onion, celery, bell pepper, mayonnaise, curry powder, lemon juice and remaining ½ teaspoon salt in large bowl; mix well.

3. Cut potatoes into 1-inch pieces. Add potatoes to yogurt mixture; stir gently to coat.

taco twist soup

Makes 4 servings

1 pound ground beef
2 teaspoons chili powder
1 teaspoon ground cumin
1¾ cups SWANSON® Beef Broth (Regular, Lower Sodium **or** Certified Organic)
1 cup PACE® Picante Sauce
1 can (14.5 ounces) diced tomatoes, undrained
1 cup **uncooked** corkscrew-shaped pasta
Sour cream

1. Cook the beef, chili powder and cumin in a 12-inch skillet over medium-high heat until the beef is well browned, stirring often to break up the meat. Pour off any fat.

2. Add the broth, picante sauce and tomatoes. Heat to a boil. Stir in the pasta. Reduce the heat to medium and cook for 15 minutes or until done, stirring occasionally. Garnish with sour cream.

waldorf brown rice salad

Makes 4 servings

1 cup MINUTE® Brown Rice, uncooked
3 medium apples
2 tablespoons lemon juice
½ cup celery, chopped
½ cup walnuts, chopped
½ cup raisins
¾ cup nonfat vanilla yogurt
½ cup fat-free mayonnaise
Spring salad greens (optional)

Prepare rice according to package directions. Cool.

Wash, core and dice apples, without peeling. Place apples in large bowl and toss with lemon juice.

Add rice, celery, walnuts and raisins; toss to combine.

Combine yogurt and mayonnaise in medium bowl. Blend well. Fold into rice mixture. Serve over salad greens, if desired.

south asian curried potato salad

mediterranean pasta salad

Makes 8 servings

- 8 ounces rotini pasta
- ½ cup WISH-BONE® Italian Dressing
- 1 tablespoon HELLMANN'S® or BEST FOODS® DIJONNAISE™ Creamy Dijon Mustard
- 1 pound boneless skinless chicken breasts, grilled and cut into bite-size pieces
- ½ cup sliced pitted ripe olives
- 1 jar (7 ounces) roasted red peppers, drained and chopped
- 1 jar (6 ounces) artichoke hearts, drained and chopped
- 2 tablespoons chopped fresh parsley (optional)

1. Cook rotini according to package directions; drain and rinse with cold water until completely cool.

2. Combine WISH-BONE® Italian Dressing with HELLMANN'S® or BEST FOODS® DIJONNAISE™ Creamy Dijon Mustard in large bowl. Add remaining ingredients; toss to coat. Chill, if desired.

Prep Time: 20 minutes
Cook Time: 20 minutes

mediterranean pasta salad

creamy roasted poblano soup

Makes 4 servings

- 6 large poblano peppers
- 1 tablespoon olive oil
- ¾ cup chopped onion
- ½ cup thinly sliced celery
- ½ cup thinly sliced carrots
- 1 clove garlic, minced
- 2 cans (about 14 ounces each) chicken broth
- 1 package (8 ounces) cream cheese, cubed
- Salt and black pepper

1. Preheat broiler. Line broiler pan or baking sheet with foil. Place poblano peppers on foil; broil 5 to 6 inches from heat source 15 minutes or until blistered and beginning to char, turning occasionally. Place peppers in medium bowl; cover bowl with plastic wrap. Let stand 20 minutes.

2. Meanwhile, heat oil in large saucepan over medium-high heat. Add onion, celery, carrots and garlic; cook and stir 4 minutes or until onion is translucent. Add broth; bring to a boil. Reduce heat to medium-low; cover and simmer 12 minutes or until celery is tender.

3. Remove skins, stems and seeds from peppers. Briefly run peppers under running water to help remove skins and seeds, if necessary. (This removes some smoky flavor, so work quickly.) Add peppers to broth mixture.

4. Working in batches, process broth mixture and cream cheese in food processor or blender until smooth; return to saucepan. Cook and stir over medium heat 2 minutes or until heated through. Season with salt and black pepper.

cool-as-a-cucumber salad

Makes 6 servings

- 4 cups cooked UNCLE BEN'S® ORIGINAL CONVERTED® Brand Rice
- 1 cup finely chopped seeded cucumber
- ¾ cup plain yogurt or sour cream
- 2 tablespoons finely chopped onion
- 1 tablespoon balsamic vinegar
- 2 teaspoons dried dill weed
- 1 teaspoon salt
- ¼ teaspoon black pepper

1. Rinse hot cooked rice under cold running water to cool; drain.

2. In large bowl, combine rice with remaining ingredients; mix well. Cover and refrigerate until well chilled to allow flavors to blend, about 4 hours.

spam® corn chowder

Makes 6 to 8 servings

- 1 cup chopped onion
- 1 tablespoon butter or margarine
- 1½ cups diced peeled potatoes
- ½ cup chopped green bell pepper
- 2 (15-ounce) cans cream-style corn
- 2 cups milk
- 1 (12-ounce) can SPAM® Classic, cubed

In 3-quart saucepan over medium heat, sauté onion in butter 5 to 10 minutes or until golden. Add potatoes and bell pepper. Cook and stir 2 minutes. Add corn and milk. Bring to a boil. Reduce heat and simmer 15 minutes or until potatoes are tender, stirring occasionally. Stir in SPAM® Classic. Simmer 2 minutes.

velvety vegetable cheese soup

velvety vegetable cheese soup

Makes 6 servings

- 1 package (16 ounces) frozen broccoli, cauliflower and carrot blend
- 2 cans (14 ounces each) fat-free reduced-sodium chicken broth
- ¾ pound (12 ounces) VELVEETA® 2% Milk Pasteurized Prepared Cheese Product, cut into ½-inch cubes

BRING combined vegetables and broth to boil in large covered saucepan on medium-high heat. Simmer on low heat 10 minutes or until vegetables are tender.

STIR in VELVEETA®; cook 5 minutes or until VELVEETA® is completely melted and soup is heated through, stirring frequently.

Tip: For a smooth consistency, soup can be puréed in a blender or food processor or right in the pan with a hand or immersion blender.

southwestern beef stew

Makes 6 servings

1 tablespoon plus 1 teaspoon BERTOLLI® Olive Oil, divided
1½ pounds boneless beef chuck, cut into 1-inch cubes
1 can (4 ounces) chopped green chiles, drained
2 large cloves garlic, finely chopped
1 teaspoon ground cumin (optional)
1 can (14 to 16 ounces) whole or plum tomatoes, undrained and chopped
1 envelope LIPTON® RECIPE SECRETS® Onion or Beefy Onion Soup Mix
1 cup water
1 package (10 ounces) frozen cut okra or green beans, thawed
1 large red or green bell pepper, cut into 1-inch pieces
4 frozen half-ears corn-on-the-cob, thawed and each cut into 3 round pieces
2 tablespoons chopped fresh cilantro

1. In 5-quart Dutch oven or heavy saucepan, heat 1 tablespoon olive oil over medium-high heat and brown half of the beef; remove and set aside. Repeat with remaining beef; remove and set aside.

2. In same Dutch oven, heat remaining 1 teaspoon olive oil over medium heat and cook chiles, garlic and cumin, stirring constantly, 3 minutes. Return beef to Dutch oven. Stir in tomatoes and soup mix blended with water. Bring to a boil over high heat. Reduce heat to low and simmer covered, stirring occasionally, 1 hour.

3. Stir in okra, bell pepper and corn. Bring to a boil over high heat. Reduce heat to low and simmer covered, stirring occasionally, 30 minutes or until meat is tender. Sprinkle with cilantro.

greek lamb salad with fresh mint dressing

Makes 4 servings

¾ pound cooked AMERICAN LAMB leg or shoulder, cut into ½-inch cubes
½ cup pitted kalamata or black olives, drained and sliced in half
⅓ cup prepared balsamic salad dressing
2 tablespoons chopped fresh mint leaves
8 cups (7-ounce package) salad greens
5 thin slices red onion, cut into rings
1 medium cucumber, thinly sliced
½ cup coarsely crumbled feta cheese

In medium bowl, combine lamb, olives, salad dressing and mint; allow to marinate for 15 minutes.

In large salad bowl, combine salad greens, red onions, cucumber and feta cheese. Add salad dressing mixture and toss to coat.

Prep Time: 15 minutes

Favorite recipe from **American Lamb Board**

Tip: This recipe is a great way to use up leftover lamb, particularly in the spring when the flavors of fresh mint, crisp cucumber and briny kalamata olives will delight your taste buds.

avocado melon salad & picante honey dressing

avocado melon salad & picante honey dressing

Makes 6 servings

½ cup PACE® Picante Sauce
3 tablespoons honey
2 tablespoons lime juice
1 tablespoon vegetable oil
3 cups fresh spinach leaves, torn into bite-sized pieces
2 cups cubed cantaloupe
1 large avocado, peeled, pitted and cut into cubes (about 1 cup)
¼ cup toasted slivered blanched almonds

1. Beat the picante sauce, honey, lime juice and oil in a large bowl with a fork or whisk.

2. Add the spinach, cantaloupe and avocado and toss to coat. Sprinkle with the almonds. Serve immediately.

Prep Time: 20 minutes
Total Time: 20 minutes

Tip: To toast the almonds, arrange the almonds in a single layer in a shallow baking pan. Bake at 350°F. for 10 minutes or until they're lightly browned.

creamy smoked turkey and blueberry salad

Makes 6 to 8 servings

- ½ cup light mayonnaise
- ½ cup plain low-fat yogurt
- ¼ cup orange marmalade
- 2 teaspoons fresh lemon juice
- ½ teaspoon ground black pepper
- 3 medium peaches (about 1 pound), cut in wedges (about 3 cups)
- 1 pint blueberries
- 2 cups cubed smoked turkey (about 8 ounces)

In a bowl, combine mayonnaise, yogurt, marmalade, lemon juice and pepper. Add peach slices, blueberries and turkey; toss until well coated. Serve on lettuce leaves, if desired.

Favorite recipe from **U.S. Highbush Blueberry Council**

refreshing strawberry soup

Makes 4 servings

- 2 cups strawberries, chilled, stems removed
- 1 cup low-fat buttermilk
- 1 tablespoon plus 1 teaspoon sugar
  Fresh mint leaves (optional)

Place all ingredients except mint in food processor; process until smooth. Serve immediately or chill before serving. Garnish with mint leaves.

Favorite recipe from **The Sugar Association, Inc.**

potato cheddar soup

Makes 6 servings

- 2 pounds new red potatoes, peeled and cut into ½-inch cubes
- ¾ cup coarsely chopped carrots
- 1 medium onion, coarsely chopped
- ½ teaspoon salt
- 3 cups chicken broth
- 1 cup half-and-half
- ¼ teaspoon black pepper
- 2 cups (8 ounces) shredded Cheddar cheese

Slow Cooker Directions

1. Place potatoes, carrots, onion and salt in **CROCK-POT®** slow cooker. Pour in broth. Cover; cook on LOW 6 to 7 hours or on HIGH 3 to 3½ hours or until vegetables are tender.

2. Turn **CROCK-POT®** slow cooker to HIGH. Stir in half-and-half and pepper. Cover; cook on HIGH 15 minutes. Turn off heat and remove cover; let stand 5 minutes. Stir in cheese until melted.

potato cheddar soup

chicken & barley soup

Makes 4 servings

- 1 cup thinly sliced celery
- 1 onion, coarsely chopped
- 1 carrot, thinly sliced
- ½ cup uncooked medium pearl barley
- 1 clove garlic, minced
- 1 cut-up whole chicken (about 3 pounds)
- 1 tablespoon olive oil
- 2½ cups chicken broth
- 1 can (about 14 ounces) diced tomatoes
- ¾ teaspoon salt
- ½ teaspoon dried basil
- ¼ teaspoon black pepper

Slow Cooker Directions

1. Place celery, onion, carrot, barley and garlic in slow cooker.

2. Remove and discard skin from chicken. Separate drumsticks from thighs. Trim back bone from breasts. Save wings for another use. Heat oil in large skillet over medium-high heat; brown chicken on all sides. Place in slow cooker.

3. Add broth, tomatoes, salt, basil and pepper to slow cooker. Cover; cook on LOW 7 to 8 hours or HIGH 4 hours or until chicken and barley are tender. Remove chicken from slow cooker; separate meat from bones. Cut into bite-size pieces, discarding bones; stir chicken into soup.

tuna dijon potato salad

Makes 8 servings

- 1½ pounds small yellow potatoes
- ½ pound fresh green beans, trimmed
- 2 pouches (4.5 ounces each) STARKIST TUNA CREATIONS®, Herb and Garlic
- 16 red cherry tomatoes, halved
- ¼ cup extra virgin olive oil
- 2 tablespoons red wine vinegar
- 2 tablespoons Dijon mustard
- 2 tablespoons capers, drained
- 2 tablespoons chopped fresh oregano
- 4 cups field greens or baby lettuce

Cook potatoes in boiling water 15 to 20 minutes, until just tender. Drain and immediately cool under running cold water.

Steam green beans in microwave until just tender, about 4 to 5 minutes. Cool immediately under running cold water or plunge in ice bath to cool.

Cut potatoes in quarters and place in a large bowl. Add green beans, tuna and tomatoes.

Place olive oil in small bowl. Whisk in vinegar and mustard until thick and creamy. Whisk in capers and oregano. Pour dressing over potato and tuna mixture and toss. Serve over field greens.

Prep Time: 15 minutes
Cook Time: 25 minutes

quinoa and shrimp salad

Makes 4 to 6 servings

- 1 cup uncooked quinoa
- 2 cups water
- ½ teaspoon salt, divided
- 1 bag (12 ounces) cooked baby shrimp, thawed and well drained
- 1 cup cherry or grape tomatoes, halved
- ¼ cup chopped fresh basil
- 2 tablespoons capers
- 2 tablespoons finely chopped green onion
- 3 tablespoons olive oil
- 1 teaspoon grated lemon peel
- 1 to 2 tablespoons lemon juice
- ⅛ teaspoon black pepper

1. Place quinoa in fine-mesh sieve. Rinse well under cold running water. Bring water and ¼ teaspoon salt to a boil in medium saucepan over high heat. Stir in quinoa. Cover; reduce heat to low. Simmer 12 to 14 minutes or until water is absorbed and quinoa is tender. Let stand 15 minutes, stirring occasionally.

2. Combine quinoa, shrimp, tomatoes, basil, capers and green onion in large bowl. Whisk oil, lemon peel and juice, pepper and remaining ¼ teaspoon salt in small bowl until blended. Pour over salad; toss gently.

quinoa and shrimp salad

spring pea & mint soup

Makes 6 servings

- 1 tablespoon butter
- 1 tablespoon vegetable oil
- 3 small leeks, whites only, cleaned and diced (about 2 cups)
- 4 cups SWANSON® Chicken Broth (Regular, Natural Goodness® or Certified Organic)
- 1 medium Yukon Gold potato, diced (about 1 cup)
- 1 package (16 ounces) frozen peas (3 cups)
- ½ cup heavy cream **or** crème fraîche
- ¼ cup thinly sliced fresh mint leaves
- 1 cup PEPPERIDGE FARM® Croutons, any variety

1. Heat the butter and oil in a 3-quart saucepan over medium heat. Add the leeks and cook until they're tender.

2. Stir in the broth and potato. Heat to a boil. Reduce the heat to low and cook for 20 minutes or until the potato is tender.

3. Stir in the peas. Cook for 10 minutes or until the peas are tender.

4. Place ⅓ of the soup mixture into an electric blender or food processor container. Cover and blend until smooth. Pour the mixture into a large bowl. Repeat the blending process twice more with the remaining broth mixture. Return all of the puréed mixture to the saucepan. Add the cream and mint. Cook over medium heat until the mixture is hot. Season to taste.

5. Divide the soup among 6 serving bowls. Top **each** serving of soup with croutons.

Prep Time: 10 minutes
Cook Time: 45 minutes

tuscan pasta salad

Makes 8 servings

- ¼ cup white balsamic vinegar
- 1 tablespoon sugar
- 1 teaspoon Italian seasoning
- ¼ teaspoon *each* salt and ground black pepper
- 1 clove garlic, minced
- ¾ cup vegetable oil
- 1 package (16 ounces) uncooked penne pasta
- 2 cups broccoli florets, coarsely chopped
- 2 cups cauliflower florets, coarsely chopped
- ½ cup sliced pitted kalamata olives
- ½ cup diced red bell pepper
- 2 tablespoons sun-dried tomatoes in oil, drained and chopped
- 2 tablespoons finely chopped fresh basil leaves
- ⅓ cup FISHER® CULINARY TOUCH™ Toasted Pine Nuts

1. In small bowl, whisk vinegar, sugar, Italian seasoning, salt, black pepper and garlic. Whisk in oil. Cover and refrigerate until ready to use.

2. Cook pasta according to package directions. Place drained pasta in large serving bowl.

3. Add broccoli, cauliflower, olives, red bell pepper, sun-dried tomatoes and basil.

4. Whisk dressing. Drizzle over salad; toss to coat. Sprinkle with pine nuts. Serve immediately.

bacon potato chowder

bacon potato chowder

Makes 8 servings

- 4 slices bacon, cooked and crumbled
- 1 large onion, chopped (about 1 cup)
- 4 cans (10¾ ounces **each**) CAMPBELL'S® Condensed Cream of Potato Soup
- 4 soup cans milk
- ¼ teaspoon ground black pepper
- 2 large russet potatoes, cut into ½-inch pieces (about 3 cups)
- ½ cup chopped fresh chives
- 2 cups shredded Cheddar cheese (about 8 ounces)

Slow Cooker Directions
1. Stir the bacon, onion, soup, milk, black pepper, potatoes and ¼ **cup** chives in a 6-quart slow cooker.

2. Cover and cook on HIGH for 3 to 4 hours or until the potatoes are tender.

3. Add the cheese and stir until the cheese is melted. Serve with the remaining chives.

winter's best bean soup

Makes 8 to 10 servings

- 6 ounces bacon, diced
- 10 cups chicken broth
- 3 cans (about 15 ounces each) Great Northern beans, drained
- 1 can (about 14 ounces) diced tomatoes
- 1 large onion, chopped
- 1 package (about 10 ounces) frozen sliced carrots
- 2 teaspoons minced garlic
- 1 fresh rosemary sprig *or* 1 teaspoon dried rosemary
- 1 teaspoon black pepper

Slow Cooker Directions

1. Cook bacon in medium skillet over medium-high heat until crisp. Drain fat. Transfer to slow cooker.

2. Add broth, beans, tomatoes, onion, carrots, garlic, rosemary sprig and black pepper.

3. Cover; cook on LOW 8 hours. Remove rosemary sprig before serving.

Prep Time: 15 minutes
Cook Time: 8 hours

Tip: This is a perfect soup to make on a cold, gray day. The bacon and beans give it a rich, hearty flavor, and it will be sure to warm you up. Serve it with thick slices of country bread drizzled with olive oil to soak up all the delicious broth.

tomato parsley salad

Makes 4 to 6 servings

- ½ cup FILIPPO BERIO® Extra Virgin Olive Oil
- 3 tablespoons white wine vinegar
- 2 cloves garlic, minced
- ¼ teaspoon salt
- ¼ teaspoon freshly ground black pepper
- 4 cups fresh parsley leaves
- ½ cup grated Parmesan cheese
- 4 tomatoes, thinly sliced

In small bowl, whisk together olive oil, vinegar, garlic, salt and pepper. Place parsley in large bowl. Add olive oil mixture and cheese; stir well. Add tomatoes; toss until lightly coated.

fiesta pasta salad

Makes 6 to 8 servings

- 12 ounces tricolor rotini pasta
- 1 cup ORTEGA® Garden Vegetable Salsa
- ¼ cup mayonnaise
- 1 cup frozen corn, thawed
- 1 cup ORTEGA® Black Beans, drained
- 2 tablespoons ORTEGA® Diced Jalapeños
- 3 green onions, diced
- ½ cup chopped fresh cilantro

COOK pasta according to package directions. Cool.

COMBINE pasta, salsa, mayonnaise, corn, beans, jalapeños, green onions and cilantro in large bowl; mix well. Refrigerate at least 30 minutes before serving.

Prep Time: 5 minutes
Start-to-Finish Time: 45 minutes

cheesy spinach soup

cheesy spinach soup

Makes 4 servings

1 tablespoon soft reduced calorie
  margarine
¼ cup chopped onions
2 cups fat-free milk
½ pound (8 ounces) VELVEETA® Made
  With 2% Milk Reduced Fat
  Pasteurized Prepared Cheese
  Product, cut into ½-inch cubes
1 package (10 ounces) frozen
  chopped spinach, cooked, well
  drained
⅛ teaspoon ground nutmeg
  Dash pepper

MELT margarine in medium saucepan
on medium heat. Add onions; cook and
stir until tender.

ADD remaining ingredients; cook on
low heat until VELVEETA® is melted
and soup is heated through, stirring
occasionally.

Prep Time: 15 minutes
Total Time: 25 minutes

zesty noodle soup

Makes 6 servings

1 pound BOB EVANS® Zesty Hot Roll
  Sausage
1 (16-ounce) can whole tomatoes,
  undrained
½ pound fresh mushrooms, sliced
1 large onion, chopped
1 small green bell pepper, chopped
2½ cups tomato juice
2½ cups water
¼ cup chopped fresh parsley
1 teaspoon lemon juice
1 teaspoon Worcestershire sauce
1 teaspoon celery seeds
½ teaspoon salt
½ teaspoon dried thyme leaves
1 cup uncooked egg noodles

Crumble sausage into 3-quart saucepan.
Cook over medium-high heat until
browned, stirring occasionally. Drain off
any drippings.

Add tomatoes with juice, mushrooms,
onion and pepper; cook until vegetables
are tender, stirring well to break up
tomatoes.

Stir in all remaining ingredients except
noodles. Bring to a boil over high heat.
Reduce heat to low; simmer, covered,
30 minutes. Add noodles; simmer just
until noodles are tender, yet firm. Serve
hot. Refrigerate leftovers.

roasted vegetable salad with capers and walnuts

Makes 6 to 8 servings

- 1 pound small Brussels sprouts
- 1 pound unpeeled small Yukon Gold potatoes
- ¼ teaspoon salt
- ¼ teaspoon black pepper
- ¼ teaspoon dried rosemary
- 5 tablespoons olive oil, divided
- 1 red bell pepper, cut into bite-size chunks
- ¼ cup walnuts, coarsely chopped
- 2 tablespoons capers
- 1½ tablespoons white wine vinegar

1. Preheat oven to 400°F. For salad, wash, trim and pat dry Brussels sprouts. Slash bottoms. Scrub and pat dry potatoes; cut into halves.

2. Place Brussels sprouts and potatoes in shallow roasting pan; sprinkle with salt, black pepper and rosemary. Drizzle with 3 tablespoons oil; toss to coat. Roast 20 minutes. Stir in bell pepper; roast 15 minutes or until vegetables are tender. Transfer to large bowl; stir in walnuts and capers.

3. Whisk remaining 2 tablespoons oil and vinegar in small bowl until blended. Pour over salad; toss to coat. Serve at room temperature.

roasted vegetable salad with capers and walnuts

german potato salad with grilled sausage

Makes 6 to 8 servings

⅔ cup prepared vinaigrette salad dressing
¼ cup **French's**® Spicy Brown Mustard or **French's**® Honey Dijon Mustard
1 tablespoon sugar
1½ pounds red or other boiling potatoes, cut into ¾-inch cubes
1 teaspoon salt
1 cup chopped green bell pepper
1 cup chopped celery
½ cup chopped onion
½ pound kielbasa or smoked sausage, split lengthwise

1. Combine salad dressing, mustard and sugar in large bowl; set aside.

2. Place potatoes in large saucepan. Add salt and enough water to cover potatoes. Heat to boiling. Cook 10 to 15 minutes until potatoes are tender. Drain and transfer to bowl with dressing. Add bell pepper, celery and onion. Set aside.

3. Grill sausage over medium-high heat until lightly browned and heated through. Cut into small cubes. Add to bowl with potatoes. Toss well to coat evenly. Serve warm.

Prep Time: 15 minutes
Cook Time: 15 minutes

manhattan clam chowder

Makes about 6 servings

¼ cup chopped bacon
1 cup chopped onion
½ cup chopped carrots
½ cup chopped celery
2 cans (14.5 ounces each) CONTADINA® Recipe Ready Diced Tomatoes, undrained
1 can (8 ounces) CONTADINA® Tomato Sauce
1 bottle (8 ounces) clam juice
1 large bay leaf
½ teaspoon chopped fresh rosemary
⅛ teaspoon black pepper
2 cans (6.5 ounces each) chopped clams, undrained

1. Sauté bacon with onion, carrots and celery in large saucepan.

2. Stir in undrained tomatoes with remaining ingredients, except clams. Heat to boiling. Reduce heat; boil gently 15 minutes. Stir in clams and juice.

3. Heat additional 5 minutes. Remove bay leaf before serving.

Microwave Directions: Combine bacon, onion, carrots and celery in 2-quart microwave-safe casserole dish. Microwave on HIGH (100%) power 5 minutes. Stir in remaining ingredients, except clams. Microwave on HIGH (100%) power 5 minutes. Stir in clams and juice. Microwave on HIGH (100%) power 5 minutes. Remove bay leaf before serving.

german potato salad with grilled sausage

very verde green bean salad

Makes 4 servings

1 tablespoon olive oil
1 pound fresh green beans
½ cup water
½ teaspoon salt
½ teaspoon black pepper
½ cup ORTEGA® Salsa Verde
2 tablespoons ORTEGA® Garden
    Vegetable Salsa

HEAT oil in large skillet over medium heat. When oil begins to shimmer, add green beans; toss lightly in oil. Heat about 3 minutes, tossing to coat beans well.

ADD water, salt and pepper carefully. Cover; cook 5 minutes or until beans are tender. Add salsas; toss to coat beans evenly. Heat 1 or 2 minutes to warm salsas. Refrigerate or serve at room temperature.

Prep Time: 5 minutes
Start-to-Finish Time: 15 minutes

creamy broccoli noodle soup

Makes 4 servings

3½ cups milk
1 package (10 ounces) frozen
    chopped broccoli
1 envelope LIPTON® Soup Secrets
    Noodle Soup Mix with Real
    Chicken Broth

1. In medium saucepan, combine all ingredients; bring to a boil.

2. Reduce heat and simmer uncovered, stirring occasionally, 5 minutes or until noodles are tender.

white cheddar cauliflower soup

Makes 8 to 10 servings

½ cup (1 stick) butter
½ cup chopped onion
½ cup all-purpose flour
½ teaspoon white pepper
3 cups milk
3 cups chicken broth
4 cups cauliflower florets
2 cups (8 ounces) shredded white
    Cheddar cheese
⅓ cup chopped fresh Italian parsley

1. Melt butter in large saucepan over medium-high heat. Add onion; cook and stir 5 minutes or until translucent. Add flour and pepper; cook 2 minutes, whisking constantly.

2. Whisk in milk and broth. Add cauliflower; bring to a boil over high heat, stirring constantly. Reduce heat to low; cover and simmer 5 minutes, stirring occasionally. Remove from heat; stir in cheese.

3. Place 4 cups soup in blender or food processor; process until smooth. Return to saucepan; cook over low heat just until thickened. Sprinkle with parsley before serving.

very verde green bean salad

creamy citrus tomato soup with pesto croutons

creamy citrus tomato soup with pesto croutons

Makes 6 servings

1 can (10¾ ounces) CAMPBELL'S®
  Condensed Tomato Soup
  (Regular **or** Healthy Request®)
1 cup milk
½ cup light cream **or** half-and-half
1 tablespoon lemon juice
6 tablespoons prepared pesto sauce
6 slices French **or** Italian bread,
  ½-inch thick, toasted

1. Stir the soup, milk, cream and lemon juice in a 2-quart saucepan. Heat over medium heat until the mixture is hot and bubbling.

2. Spread **1 tablespoon** pesto on **each** toast slice.

3. Divide the soup among **6** serving bowls. Float **1** pesto crouton in **each** bowl of soup.

Prep Time: 10 minutes
Cook Time: 5 minutes

Tip: If you have some goat cheese on hand, spread a little on the toast slices before topping with the pesto.

chipotle peach salad

Makes 5 servings

2 pounds boneless skinless chicken
  breasts
  Salt and pepper
1 canned chipotle pepper in adobo
  sauce
1½ tablespoons adobo sauce from
  chipotle can, divided
2 ripe SUMMERWHITE® or yellow
  peaches, divided
3 tablespoons olive oil
3 tablespoons fresh lime juice
½ teaspoon salt
½ teaspoon sugar
1 bag hearts of romaine lettuce
½ cup quartered and thinly sliced
  red onion
½ cup coarsely crushed white
  tortilla chips

1. Rinse chicken breasts and pat dry. Sprinkle with salt and pepper and brush with 1 tablespoon adobo sauce. Grill over medium coals for about 5 minutes per side or until charred and cooked through. Chill, and then cut into small bite-size strips.

2. Meanwhile, peel and pit one of the peaches. Transfer to a blender container with the chipotle pepper, the remaining adobo sauce, olive oil, lime juice, salt and sugar; blend until smooth. Pit and thinly slice the remaining peach and place in a large salad bowl with the chicken, romaine and onion. Drizzle with dressing and toss well to coat. Top with tortilla chips.

Prep Time: 15 minutes
Cook Time: 10 to 15 minutes
Chill Time: 30 minutes

Favorite recipe from **California Tree Fruit Agreement**

beet and goat cheese salad

Makes 4 servings

1 pound whole beets with greens
3 quarts water
2⅛ teaspoons salt, divided
  Spring greens (optional)
2 tablespoons red wine vinegar
1 teaspoon Dijon mustard
¼ teaspoon black pepper
¼ cup extra virgin olive oil
¼ cup canola oil
½ cup chopped hazelnuts
4 ounces goat cheese

1. Slice off beet greens; reserve. Bring water and 2 teaspoons salt to a boil in large saucepan. Add beets; cook 20 to 25 minutes or until crisp-tender. Drain. Peel beets under running water to help prevent staining your fingers. Drain. Cut each beet into 8 equal pieces. Transfer to large bowl.

2. Thoroughly wash beet greens. Remove and discard tough stems. Tear greens into large pieces. Add spring greens, if necessary, to make 6 cups. Place greens in bowl with beets.

3. For dressing, whisk vinegar, mustard, pepper and remaining ⅛ teaspoon salt in small bowl until blended. Slowly drizzle in olive oil and canola oil, whisking constantly.

4. Toast hazelnuts in small skillet over medium heat 5 minutes or until golden brown. Transfer to medium bowl; cool slightly. Stir in goat cheese. Form teaspoonfuls cheese mixture into balls. Toss beets and greens with dressing. Top with cheese balls.

Note: The beets, dressing and cheese balls can be prepared in advance. Assemble salad just before serving.

roasted squash soup with crispy bacon

Makes 6 servings

1 small butternut squash (about
    1½ pounds), diced (about 4 cups)
2 large onions, sliced (about 2 cups)
3 tablespoons olive oil
3 cups SWANSON® Chicken Broth
    (Regular, Natural Goodness® or
    Certified Organic)
½ cup heavy cream
¼ cup real bacon bits

1. Heat the oven to 425°F. Place the squash and onions in a 17×11-inch roasting pan. Add the oil and toss to coat. Bake for 25 minutes or until the squash is tender.

2. Place ½ of the squash mixture, 1½ **cups** of the broth and ¼ **cup** of the cream in an electric blender or food processor container. Cover and blend until smooth. Pour the mixture into a medium bowl. Repeat the blending process with the remaining squash mixture, broth and cream. Season to taste. Return all of the puréed mixture to a 3-quart saucepan. Cook over medium heat for 5 minutes or until hot.

3. Divide the soup among **6** serving bowls. Top **each** serving of soup with **2 teaspoons** of the bacon.

beet and goat cheese salad

shrimp and pepper bisque

Makes 4 servings

- 1 bag (12 ounces) frozen stir-fry vegetables, thawed
- 8 ounces frozen cauliflower florets, thawed
- 1 stalk celery, sliced
- 1 tablespoon seafood seasoning
- ½ teaspoon dried thyme
- 1 can (about 14 ounces) chicken broth
- 12 ounces medium raw shrimp, peeled
- 2 cups half-and-half
- 2 to 3 green onions, finely chopped

Slow Cooker Directions

1. Combine stir-fry vegetables, cauliflower, celery, seasoning and thyme in slow cooker. Pour in broth. Cover; cook on LOW 8 hours or on HIGH 4 hours.

2. Stir in shrimp. Cover; cook 15 minutes or until shrimp are pink and opaque. Working in batches, process mixture in food processor or blender until smooth; return to slow cooker. Stir in half-and-half. Sprinkle with green onions just before serving.

Prep Time: 10 minutes
Cook Time: 8¼ hours (LOW) or 4¼ hours (HIGH)

Tip: For a creamier, smoother consistency, strain through several layers of damp cheesecloth.

watermelon hawaiian salad

Makes 8 to 12 servings

- 1 cup macadamia nuts
- 2 bananas
- 1 small papaya
  Juice from 4 limes
- 3 cups seedless watermelon balls or small squares
- 2 cups fresh pineapple chunks
- 1 cup freshly grated or unsweetened coconut
- 3 cups low-fat vanilla flavored yogurt
- ⅓ cup papaya seeds

1. Place macadamia nuts in food processor fitted with steel blade and pulse to chop into large pieces. Transfer nuts to nonstick heavy skillet and toast over medium heat just until golden, stirring constantly. Remove to heatproof dish or bowl and allow to cool.

2. Peel and cut bananas and papaya into small chunks, place in large bowl and toss with lime juice. Add watermelon, pineapple and coconut. In another bowl, stir together yogurt and papaya seeds. Pour over fruit mixture. Toss to combine. Sprinkle toasted macadamia nuts over top and serve immediately.

Favorite recipe from **National Watermelon Promotion Board**

spinach salad with grilled chicken thighs

Makes 4 servings

1¼ cups WISH-BONE® Italian or Robusto Italian Dressing
⅓ cup finely chopped, drained sun-dried tomatoes packed in oil
4 tablespoons grated Parmesan cheese
1½ pounds boneless, skinless chicken thighs
1 cup sliced baby portobellas, cremini and/or white mushrooms
½ small red onion, thinly sliced
1 package (10 ounces) fresh spinach leaves, trimmed, rinsed and patted dry

1. For marinade, combine WISH-BONE® Italian Dressing, tomatoes and 2 tablespoons cheese. In large, shallow nonaluminum baking dish or plastic bag, pour ½ cup marinade over chicken; turn to coat. Cover, or close bag, and marinate in refrigerator, turning occasionally, up to 3 hours. Refrigerate remaining marinade.

2. Remove chicken from marinade, discarding marinade. Grill or broil chicken, turning once and brushing frequently with ¼ cup refrigerated marinade, until chicken is thoroughly cooked. To serve, slice chicken. Arrange chicken, mushrooms and onion over spinach; drizzle with remaining refrigerated marinade. Sprinkle with remaining 2 tablespoons cheese and, if desired, cracked black pepper.

easy beef taco salad

Makes 6 servings

1 pound ground beef
1 small onion, chopped
1 package (1¼ ounces) TACO BELL® HOME ORIGINALS® Taco Seasoning Mix
¾ cup water
1 package (10 ounces) frozen corn
½ pound (8 ounces) VELVEETA® Pasteurized Prepared Cheese Product, cut into ½-inch cubes
1 bag (8 ounces) shredded iceberg lettuce (about 4½ cups)
1 large tomato, chopped
6 ounces tortilla chips (about 9 cups)

BROWN meat with onions in large skillet on medium-high heat; drain. Add seasoning mix and water; cook as directed on package.

STIR in corn and VELVEETA®; cover. Cook on low heat 5 minutes or until VELVEETA® is completely melted and mixture is well blended, stirring frequently.

SPOON over lettuce just before serving; top with tomatoes. Serve with tortilla chips.

Prep Time: 10 minutes
Total Time: 30 minutes

Tip: Iceberg lettuce was developed in the 1920s by producers who wanted a less perishable lettuce that would withstand cross-country shipping. It has a mild taste, crisp texture and pale green color. It keeps well.

spinach salad with grilled chicken thighs

wild rice salad with whole wheat pitas

wild rice salad with whole wheat pitas

Makes 6 to 8 servings

2½ cups water
¼ teaspoon salt
⅔ cup wild rice
4 ounces hard salami, cut into
    ¼-inch pieces
½ cup sliced pitted green olives
1 stalk celery, finely chopped
1 green onion, finely chopped
1 tablespoon olive oil
    Grated peel of 1 lemon
⅛ teaspoon black pepper
6 to 8 whole wheat pita bread
    rounds

1. Bring water and salt to a boil in medium saucepan over high heat. Stir in wild rice. Cover; reduce heat to low. Cook 45 minutes or until tender. Drain well; set aside to cool.

2. Spoon wild rice into large bowl. Stir in salami, olives, celery, green onion, oil, lemon peel and pepper.

3. Preheat oven to 400°F. Cut pitas into wedges. Place on baking sheet. Toast 5 minutes just before serving with salad.

Tip: Wild rice should be thoroughly rinsed before cooking to remove any debris. To rinse, place in a bowl with cold water then stir. Let stand until any debris floats to the surface. Discard the debris and drain.

smoked sausage and navy bean soup

Makes 8 servings

8 cups chicken broth
1 pound dried navy beans, sorted and rinsed
2 ham hocks (about 1 pound total)
2 onions, diced
1 cup diced carrots
1 cup diced celery
1 can (about 14 ounces) diced tomatoes, undrained
2 tablespoons tomato paste
2 cloves garlic, minced
1 bay leaf
1 teaspoon dried thyme
1 smoked sausage (1 pound), cut into ½-inch rounds

Slow Cooker Directions

1. Bring broth to a boil in large saucepan over medium-high heat. Cover; reduce heat to low.

2. Place beans in **CROCK-POT®** slow cooker. Add ham hocks, onions, carrots, celery, tomatoes, tomato paste, garlic, bay leaf and thyme. Carefully pour in hot broth. Cover; cook on HIGH 8 to 9 hours or until beans are tender.

3. Remove and discard bay leaf. Remove ham hocks from **CROCK-POT®** slow cooker; let stand until cool enough to handle. Remove ham from hocks, chop and add back to **CROCK-POT®** slow cooker. Stir in sausage. Cover; cook 15 to 30 minutes or until sausage is heated through.

tomato-lentil soup

Makes about 8 servings

2 tablespoons olive oil
2 cups chopped onion
1 cup sliced celery
1 carrot, peeled, sliced
6 cups water
1 cup dry lentils
1 can (6 ounces) CONTADINA® Tomato Paste
½ cup dry red wine or chicken broth
¼ cup chopped fresh parsley or 1 tablespoon dried parsley flakes
3 small chicken bouillon cubes
1 teaspoon salt
½ teaspoon Worcestershire sauce
¼ teaspoon black pepper
Shredded or grated Parmesan cheese (optional)

1. Heat oil over medium-high heat in large saucepan. Add onion, celery and carrot; sauté until vegetables are tender.

2. Stir in water, lentils, tomato paste, wine, parsley, bouillon cubes, salt, Worcestershire sauce and pepper. Bring to a boil.

3. Reduce heat to low; simmer, uncovered, 45 to 50 minutes or until lentils are tender. Sprinkle with Parmesan cheese, if desired.

smoked sausage and navy bean soup

pesto rice salad

pesto rice salad

Makes 6 servings

2 cups MINUTE® White Rice, uncooked
1 package (7 ounces) basil pesto sauce
1 cup cherry tomatoes, halved
8 ounces whole-milk mozzarella cheese, cut into ½-inch cubes
⅓ cup Parmesan cheese, shredded
Toasted pine nuts (optional)

Prepare rice according to package directions. Place in large bowl. Let stand 10 minutes.

Add pesto sauce; mix well. Gently stir in tomatoes and cheese.

Serve warm or cover and refrigerate until ready to serve. Sprinkle with pine nuts, if desired.

Tip: To toast pine nuts, spread in single layer in heavy skillet. Cook over medium heat 2 minutes, stirring frequently, until nuts are lightly browned. Remove from skillet immediately. Cool before using.

simple snow peas & mushroom salad

Makes 5 servings

½ cup WISH-BONE® Italian or Light Italian Dressing
1 package (8 ounces) snow peas, trimmed
1 cup sliced mushrooms
1 medium red bell pepper, cut into strips
1 package (5 ounces) mixed salad greens

1. Combine all ingredients except salad greens in large bowl. Cover and marinate in refrigerator, stirring occasionally, at least 30 minutes.

2. Arrange salad greens on serving platter, then top with marinated vegetables.

pasta fagioli

Makes 4 servings

1 jar (1 pound 10 ounces) RAGÚ® Chunky Gardenstyle Pasta Sauce
1 can (19 ounces) white kidney beans, rinsed and drained
1 box (10 ounces) frozen chopped spinach, thawed
8 ounces ditalini pasta, cooked and drained (reserve 2 cups pasta water)

1. In 6-quart saucepot, combine Pasta Sauce, beans, spinach, pasta and reserved pasta water; heat through.

2. Season, if desired, with salt, ground black pepper and grated Parmesan cheese.

Prep Time: 20 minutes
Cook Time: 10 minutes

side
dishes

side dishes

• • • • •

easy summer vegetable medley

Makes 4 to 6 servings

2 medium red or green bell peppers, cut into chunks

2 medium zucchini or summer squash, sliced lengthwise in half and then into thick slices

1 (12-ounce) package mushrooms, cleaned and cut into quarters

3 carrots, thinly sliced

1⅓ cups *French's*® French Fried Onions or *French's*® Cheddar French Fried Onions

¼ cup fresh basil, minced

2 tablespoons olive oil

Salt and black pepper to taste

2 ice cubes

1 large foil oven roasting bag

1. Toss all ingredients in large bowl. Open foil bag; spoon mixture into bag in even layer. Seal bag with tight double folds. Place bag on baking sheet.

2. Place bag on grill over medium-high heat. Cover grill and cook 15 minutes until vegetables are tender, turning bag over once.

3. Return bag to baking sheet and carefully cut top of bag open. Sprinkle with additional French Fried Onions, if desired.

Prep Time: 10 minutes
Cook Time: 15 minutes

classic coleslaw

Makes 12 servings

1 cup HELLMANN'S® or BEST
  FOODS® Real Mayonnaise*
3 tablespoons lemon juice
2 tablespoons sugar
1 teaspoon salt
6 cups shredded cabbage
1 cup shredded carrots
½ cup chopped green bell pepper

*Also terrific with HELLMANN'S® or BEST FOODS® Light or Canola Cholesterol Free Mayonnaise.

Combine HELLMANN'S® or BEST FOODS® Real Mayonnaise, lemon juice, sugar and salt in large bowl. Stir in cabbage, carrots and bell pepper. Chill, if desired.

Prep Time: 10 minutes

oven roasted tomatoes

Makes 4 servings

6 ripe plum or vine tomatoes
1 teaspoon freeze-dried oregano
2 cloves garlic, crushed
  Salt and freshly ground black
  pepper
5 tablespoons FILIPPO BERIO®
  Olive Oil

Preheat the oven to 375°F. Cut the tomatoes in half and place cut side up in a single layer, in a large oven-proof dish. Scatter the oregano, garlic and plenty of salt and pepper over the tomatoes. Drizzle with the olive oil. Bake for 30 to 35 minutes or until the tomatoes have softened.

fiery creamed spinach

Makes 4 servings

1 tablespoon olive oil
1 onion, sliced
1 bag (12 ounces) spinach, washed
  and chopped
¾ cup milk
1 packet (1.25 ounces) ORTEGA®
  Hot and Spicy Taco Seasoning
  Mix

HEAT oil in large skillet over medium heat. Add onion. Cook and stir 4 minutes or until translucent.

ADD spinach. Cook and stir until spinach begins to wilt. Stir in milk and seasoning mix. Cook and stir 4 minutes or until sauce thickens. Serve warm.

cheesy corn and peppers

Makes 8 servings

2 pounds frozen corn
2 poblano peppers, chopped
2 tablespoons butter, cubed
1 teaspoon salt
½ teaspoon ground cumin
¼ teaspoon black pepper
1 cup (4 ounces) shredded sharp
  Cheddar cheese
3 ounces cream cheese, cubed

Slow Cooker Directions
1. Coat slow cooker with nonstick cooking spray. Add corn, poblano peppers, butter, salt, cumin and black pepper. Cover; cook on HIGH 2 hours.

2. Add Cheddar cheese and cream cheese; stir to blend. Cover; cook 15 minutes or until cheeses are melted.

mexican mashed potatoes

mexican mashed potatoes

Makes 6 servings

3 pounds russet potatoes, peeled and diced
4 tablespoons (½ stick) butter
¼ cup milk
1 can (4 ounces) ORTEGA® Fire-Roasted Diced Green Chiles
Salt and black pepper, to taste
1 packet (1.25 ounces) ORTEGA® Taco Seasoning Mix

BRING large saucepot of salted water to a boil. Add potatoes. Cook 10 minutes or until soft. Drain water from pot.

ADD butter, milk, chiles, salt and pepper to taste. Mash well. Stir in seasoning mix. Serve warm.

Prep Time: 5 minutes
Start-to-Finish Time: 25 minutes

Tip: For an even richer side dish, stir in 1 cup shredded Cheddar or Monterey Jack cheese.

sautéed snow peas & baby carrots

Makes 2 servings

1 tablespoon I CAN'T BELIEVE IT'S NOT BUTTER!® Spread
2 tablespoons chopped shallots or onion
5 ounces frozen whole baby carrots, partially thawed
4 ounces snow peas (about 1 cup)
2 teaspoons chopped fresh parsley (optional)

In 12-inch nonstick skillet, melt I Can't Believe It's Not Butter!® Spread over medium heat and cook shallots, stirring occasionally, 1 minute or until almost tender. Add carrots and snow peas and cook, stirring occasionally, 4 minutes or until crisp-tender. Stir in parsley, if desired, and heat through.

rice pilaf greek style

Makes 4 to 6 servings

2 cups chicken broth, beef broth or water
1 cup uncooked long grain rice
1 tablespoon FILIPPO BERIO® Extra Virgin Olive Oil
Salt and freshly ground black pepper
Grated Parmesan or Romano cheese (optional)
Toasted pine nuts (optional)

In 3-quart saucepan, combine chicken broth, rice and olive oil. Bring to a boil over medium-high heat; stir once. Cover; reduce heat to low and simmer 15 minutes or until rice is tender and liquid is absorbed. Remove from heat; let stand, covered, 5 to 10 minutes. Season to taste with salt and pepper. Serve plain, or topped with cheese or pine nuts, if desired.

creamy corn and vegetable orzo

Makes 6 servings

2 tablespoons butter
4 medium green onions, sliced (about ½ cup)
2 cups frozen whole kernel corn
1 package (10 ounces) frozen vegetables (chopped broccoli, peas, sliced carrots **or** cut green beans)
½ of a 16-ounce package rice-shaped pasta (orzo), cooked and drained
1 can (10¾ ounces) CAMPBELL'S® Condensed Cream of Celery Soup (Regular **or** 98% Fat Free)
½ cup water

1. Heat the butter in a 12-inch skillet over medium heat. Add the green onions and cook until tender. Add the corn, vegetables and pasta. Cook and stir for 3 minutes.

2. Stir the soup and water into the skillet. Cook and stir for 5 minutes or until mixture is hot and bubbling. Serve immediately.

Prep Time: 10 minutes
Cook Time: 10 minutes

Tip: The word "orzo" actually means barley, even though the shape of this pasta looks more like rice. Orzo is an excellent base for meat or vegetable dishes, a welcome addition to soups and salads, and an ideal stuffing for tomatoes and peppers.

artichokes with lemon-tarragon butter

Makes 2 servings

6 cups water
2¼ teaspoons salt, divided
2 whole artichokes, stems cut off and leaf tips trimmed
¼ cup (½ stick) unsalted butter
¼ teaspoon grated lemon peel
2 tablespoons lemon juice
¼ teaspoon dried tarragon

1. Bring water and 2 teaspoons salt to a boil in large saucepan over high heat. Add artichokes; return to a boil. Reduce heat to medium-low; cover and simmer 35 to 45 minutes or until leaves detach easily (cooking time will depend on artichoke size).

2. Turn artichokes upside down to drain well.

3. Combine butter, lemon peel and juice, tarragon and remaining ¼ teaspoon salt in small saucepan. Cook over medium heat until melted and bubbly. Serve in small bowls alongside artichokes.

artichokes with lemon-tarragon butter

garden potato casserole

garden potato casserole

Makes 5 servings

1¼ pounds unpeeled baking potatoes, thinly sliced

1 green or red bell pepper, thinly sliced

¼ cup finely chopped yellow onion

2 tablespoons butter, cut into pieces, divided

½ teaspoon dried thyme
Salt and black pepper

1 yellow squash, thinly sliced

1 cup (4 ounces) shredded sharp Cheddar cheese

Slow Cooker Directions

1. Place potatoes, bell pepper, onion, 1 tablespoon butter and thyme in slow cooker. Season with salt and black pepper; mix well. Layer squash over top; add remaining 1 tablespoon butter.

2. Cover; cook on LOW 7 hours or on HIGH 4 hours.

3. Transfer to serving bowl. Sprinkle with cheese; let stand 2 to 3 minutes or until cheese is melted.

Prep Time: 15 minutes
Cook Time: 7 hours (LOW) or 4 hours (HIGH)

grilled leeks with orange

Makes 4 to 6 servings

- 6 large leeks
- ⅓ cup fresh orange juice
- 3 tablespoons *French's*® Spicy Brown Mustard
- 2 tablespoons reduced-sodium soy sauce
- 1 tablespoon olive oil
- 1 tablespoon *Frank's*® *RedHot*® Original Cayenne Pepper Sauce
- 2 teaspoons grated orange peel
- 1 teaspoon sugar

1. Trim off all but 1 inch green portion from leeks; discard green tops. Trim off and discard roots. Cut leeks in half lengthwise. Rinse well under cold running water to remove sand between leaves, taking care not to separate leaves from root end.

2. Place leeks and ¼ cup water in shallow microwavable dish. Cover with vented plastic wrap and microwave on HIGH (100%) 2 minutes or until leeks are crisp-tender, turning once. Drain.

3. Combine orange juice, mustard, soy sauce, oil, *Frank's RedHot* Sauce, orange peel and sugar in small bowl. Brush mixture on leeks. Place leeks in grilling basket. Grill over medium-high heat 5 to 8 minutes or until leeks are tender and golden brown, turning and basting often with mustard mixture.

Tip: Leeks are related to onions and garlic, although they are milder in flavor. Look for small to medium leeks; larger ones are not as tender. Choose leeks with firm bright green stalks and white blemish-free bases.

saucy asparagus casserole

Makes 6 servings

- 2 pounds asparagus, trimmed
- 1 can (10¾ ounces) CAMPBELL'S® Condensed Cream of Asparagus Soup
- ⅓ cup milk **or** water
- ½ cup dry bread crumbs
- 2 tablespoons butter, melted

1. Place the asparagus in a 13×9-inch shallow baking dish.

2. Stir the soup and milk in a small bowl and pour over the asparagus. Mix the bread crumbs with the butter in a small bowl and sprinkle over the soup mixture.

3. Bake at 400°F. for 20 minutes or until golden brown and bubbly.

Easy Substitution: Use 2 packages (about 10 ounces each) thawed frozen asparagus spears for the fresh asparagus.

Prep Time: 5 minutes
Bake Time: 20 minutes

saucy asparagus casserole

cheesy chipotle vegetable bake

Makes 10 servings

- 4 cups small cauliflower florets
- 4 large zucchini, sliced
- 3 medium carrots, sliced
- 2 tablespoons chopped chipotle peppers in adobo sauce
- ¼ cup KRAFT® Zesty Italian Dressing
- ½ pound (8 ounces) VELVEETA® Pasteurized Prepared Cheese Product, thinly sliced
- 20 RITZ® Crackers, crushed
- 2 tablespoons butter or margarine, melted

HEAT oven to 375°F. Combine first 5 ingredients; spoon into 13×9-inch baking dish. Top with VELVEETA®.

MIX cracker crumbs and butter; sprinkle over vegetable mixture.

BAKE 30 to 35 minutes or until vegetables are tender and casserole is heated through.

Prep Time: 15 minutes
Total Time: 45 to 50 minutes

lipton® california mashed potatoes

Makes about 4 servings

- 2 pounds all-purpose potatoes, peeled, if desired, and cut into chunks
  Water
- 1 envelope LIPTON® RECIPE SECRETS® Onion Soup Mix*
- ¾ cup milk, warmed
- ½ cup sour cream
- 2 tablespoons chopped fresh parsley (optional)

*Also terrific with LIPTON® RECIPE SECRETS® Golden Onion or Savory Herb with Garlic Soup Mix.

1. In 3-quart saucepan, cover potatoes with water. Bring to a boil over high heat. Reduce heat to low and simmer 20 minutes or until potatoes are very tender; drain.

2. Return potatoes to saucepan. Mash potatoes. Stir in soup mix blended with milk, sour cream and parsley.

brown sugar roasted carrots

Makes 8 servings

- REYNOLDS WRAP® Non-Stick Foil
- 1 package (32 ounces) peeled baby carrots
- ½ cup packed dark brown sugar
- 1 tablespoon butter, melted
- 1 teaspoon grated orange peel
- ½ teaspoon 5-spice powder
- ½ teaspoon salt
- ½ cup pecan pieces
  Orange peel (optional)

Preheat oven to 500°F. Line a 15×10×1-inch baking pan with Reynolds Wrap Non-Stick Foil with non-stick (dull) side toward food.

Place carrots in a single layer in foil-lined pan. Combine brown sugar, butter, orange peel, 5-spice powder and salt in a small bowl. Sprinkle brown sugar mixture evenly over carrots.

Bake 20 minutes, stirring once. Sprinkle with pecans; bake 2 minutes longer or until carrots are tender and glazed. Garnish with more orange peel, if desired.

Prep Time: 8 minutes
Cook Time: 22 minutes

cheesy chipotle vegetable bake

eggplant tomato gratin

eggplant tomato gratin

Makes 8 servings

Vegetable cooking spray
1 large eggplant (about 1¼ pounds)
   cut into ½-inch-thick slices
1 can (10¾ ounces) CAMPBELL'S®
   Condensed Cream of Celery
   Soup (Regular **or** 98% Fat Free)
½ cup milk
¼ cup grated Parmesan cheese
2 large tomatoes, cut into ½-inch-
   thick slices (about 2 cups)
1 medium onion, thinly sliced
   (about ½ cup)
¼ cup chopped fresh basil leaves
¼ cup Italian-seasoned dry bread
   crumbs
1 tablespoon chopped fresh parsley
   (optional)
1 tablespoon olive oil

1. Heat the oven to 425°F. Spray a
baking sheet with cooking spray.
Arrange the eggplant in a single layer.
Bake for 20 minutes or until tender,
turning halfway through baking. Spray
3-quart shallow baking dish with
cooking spray.

2. Stir the soup, milk and cheese in a
small bowl.

3. Layer **half** the eggplant, tomatoes,
onion, basil and soup mixture in the
prepared dish. Repeat the layers.

4. Stir the bread crumbs, parsley and oil
in a small bowl. Sprinkle over the soup
mixture.

5. Reduce the heat to 400°F. and bake
for 25 minutes or until hot and golden
brown. Let stand for 10 minutes.

pesto rice and beans

Makes 8 servings

1 can (about 15 ounces) Great
   Northern beans, rinsed and
   drained
1 can (about 14 ounces) chicken
   broth
¾ cup uncooked long grain white rice
1½ cups frozen cut green beans,
   thawed and drained
½ cup prepared pesto
   Grated Parmesan cheese (optional)

Slow Cooker Directions

1. Combine Great Northern beans,
broth and rice in slow cooker. Cover;
cook on LOW 2 hours.

2. Stir in green beans. Cover; cook
1 hour or until rice and beans are
tender.

3. Turn off slow cooker and remove
insert to heatproof surface. Stir in
pesto and Parmesan cheese, if desired.
Let stand, covered, 5 minutes or until
cheese is melted. Serve immediately.

Prep Time: 5 minutes
Cook Time: 3 hours

sun-dried tomato risotto

Makes 4 servings

1 jar (8 ounces) oil-packed sun-dried
  tomatoes
1½ cups **uncooked** Arborio rice **or**
  regular long grain white rice
4 cups SWANSON® Chicken Broth
  (Regular, Natural Goodness™,
  or Certified Organic), heated
1 cup frozen peas, thawed
¼ cup walnuts, toasted and chopped

1. Drain the tomatoes, reserving
2 tablespoons oil. Chop enough
tomatoes to make ½ **cup.**

2. Heat the reserved oil in a 3-quart
saucepan over medium heat. Add the
tomatoes and rice and cook and stir for
2 minutes.

3. Add **1 cup** broth and cook and stir
until it's absorbed. Add the remaining
broth, ½ **cup** at a time, stirring until
it's absorbed before adding more. Stir in
the peas and walnuts with the last broth
addition.

4. Remove the saucepan from the heat.
Cover and let stand for 5 minutes.

Tip: To quickly thaw the peas, place
them in a colander and run under
warm water.

delicious parsnip casserole

Makes 4 to 6 servings

2 pounds parsnips, peeled and sliced
1 cup (4 ounces) shredded sharp
  Cheddar cheese
⅔ cup evaporated milk
¼ cup saltine cracker crumbs
6 slices bacon, crisp-cooked and
  crumbled
1 egg, well beaten
1½ teaspoons prepared horseradish
1 teaspoon salt
¼ teaspoon black pepper

Slow Cooker Directions

1. Place parsnips in large saucepan.
Cover with water by 1 inch. Bring to a
boil over high heat; cook 15 minutes
or until tender. Drain well. Mash with
potato masher until creamy. Add
remaining ingredients; blend well.

2. Butter slow cooker; add mixture.
Cover; cook on LOW 4 to 5 hours.

Prep Time: 30 minutes
Cook Time: 4 to 5 hours

sun-dried tomato risotto

red cabbage and fruit slaw

Makes 8 servings

2 cups shredded savoy cabbage
⅓ cup shredded carrot
⅓ cup dried apricots, cut into thin
    matchstick strips
⅓ cup thin apple strips
½ cup mayonnaise
3 tablespoons cider vinegar
1 to 3 tablespoons sugar
2 cups shredded red cabbage

1. Combine savoy cabbage, carrot, apricots and apple in large bowl; mix well.

2. Combine mayonnaise, vinegar and sugar in small bowl until well blended. Pour over cabbage mixture; toss to coat. Refrigerate at least 1 hour before serving. Just before serving, stir in red cabbage.

garlic ranch whipped potatoes

Makes 6 servings

3 pounds all-purpose potatoes,
    peeled, if desired, and cubed
½ cup WISH-BONE® Garlic Ranch
    Dressing
½ cup chopped green onions
½ teaspoon salt (optional)
½ teaspoon ground black pepper

1. In 3-quart saucepan, cover potatoes with water. Bring to a boil over high heat. Reduce heat to low and simmer uncovered 20 minutes or until potatoes are very tender; drain.

2. Return potatoes to saucepan. With electric mixer or potato masher, mash until smooth. Stir in remaining ingredients.

golden corn pudding

Makes 4 to 6 servings

2 tablespoons butter or margarine
3 tablespoons all-purpose flour
1 can (14¾ ounces) DEL MONTE®
    Cream Style Golden Sweet Corn
¼ cup yellow cornmeal
2 eggs, separated
1 package (3 ounces) cream cheese,
    softened
1 can (8¾ ounces) DEL MONTE
    Whole Kernel Golden Sweet
    Corn, drained

1. Preheat oven to 350°F.

2. Melt butter in medium saucepan. Add flour and stir until smooth. Blend in cream style corn and cornmeal. Bring to a boil over medium heat, stirring constantly.

3. Place egg yolks in small bowl; stir in ½ cup hot mixture. Pour mixture back into saucepan. Add cream cheese and whole kernel corn.

4. Place egg whites in clean narrow bowl and beat until stiff peaks form. With rubber spatula, gently fold egg whites into corn mixture.

5. Pour mixture into 1½-quart straight-sided baking dish. Bake 30 to 35 minutes or until lightly browned.

Prep Time: 10 minutes
Bake Time: 35 minutes

Tip: Pudding can be prepared up to 3 hours ahead of serving time. Cover and refrigerate until about 30 minutes before baking.

red cabbage and fruit slaw

zucchini al forno

Makes 4 to 6 servings

1 tablespoon olive oil
3 small zucchini (1 pound), thinly sliced
1 package (12 ounces) mushrooms, wiped clean and thinly sliced
1 jar (14 ounces) marinara sauce
1⅓ cups *French's*® French Fried Onions, divided
½ cup ricotta cheese
⅓ cup grated Parmesan cheese
¼ cup milk
1 egg

1. Preheat oven to 375°F. Grease 2-quart oblong baking dish. Heat oil in large nonstick skillet. Add zucchini and mushrooms; cook and stir about 3 minutes or until crisp-tender. Stir in marinara sauce and ⅔ *cup* French Fried Onions. Pour into prepared baking dish.

2. Combine cheeses, milk and egg in medium bowl; mix until well blended. Spread cheese mixture over vegetable mixture.

3. Bake, uncovered, 30 minutes or until cheese layer is set. Sprinkle with remaining ⅔ *cup* onions. Bake 3 minutes or until onions are golden.

Prep Time: 15 minutes
Cook Time: 36 minutes

broccoli-stuffed tomatoes

broccoli-stuffed tomatoes

Makes 4 servings

4 large tomatoes (about 1 pound)
1 package (10 ounces) frozen chopped broccoli, thawed and well drained
⅔ cup OLD FASHIONED QUAKER® Oats, uncooked
½ cup low-fat small-curd cottage cheese
¼ cup chopped onion
1½ teaspoons minced fresh basil or ½ teaspoon dried basil leaves
1 clove garlic, minced
¼ cup finely shredded Parmesan or Swiss cheese

1. Heat oven to 350°F. Slice ¼ inch from stem end of each tomato. Scoop out pulp and seeds; discard or reserve for another use. Arrange tomatoes in shallow 1-quart glass baking dish.

2. Combine broccoli, oats, cottage cheese, onion, basil and garlic in medium bowl; mix well. Fill tomatoes with mixture; sprinkle with cheese.

3. Bake 20 to 25 minutes or until heated through.

Tip: Old fashioned and quick-cooking oats are interchangeable in most recipes. They are essentially the same, except quick-cooking oats cook faster because they have been rolled into thinner flakes. Some people prefer old fashioned oats because the thicker flakes have a heartier texture and are more flavorful. Do not substitute instant oats.

easy "baked" beans

Makes 6 servings

2 slices bacon, chopped
2 cans (19 ounces each) red kidney
   beans and/or cannellini beans,
   rinsed and drained
1 envelope LIPTON® RECIPE
   SECRETS® Beefy Onion Soup Mix
1½ cups water
¼ cup ketchup
2 tablespoons firmly packed brown
   sugar

1. In 3-quart saucepan, cook bacon over medium-high heat until crisp-tender. Stir in beans. Cook, stirring frequently, 1 minute.

2. Stir in remaining ingredients. Bring to a boil over high heat.

3. Reduce heat to medium-low and simmer uncovered, 20 minutes or until thickened.

Prep Time: 5 minutes
Cook Time: 30 minutes

spinach mediterranean style

Makes 3 to 4 servings

1 pound fresh spinach, washed,
   drained and stems removed
2 tablespoons FILIPPO BERIO®
   Olive Oil
1 clove garlic, minced
1 teaspoon balsamic or wine vinegar

Microwave Directions

Place spinach in microwave-safe 8- or 9-inch square baking dish. Drizzle with olive oil; sprinkle with garlic. Cover with vented plastic wrap. Microwave on HIGH 5 minutes or until spinach is wilted, stirring halfway through cooking. Sprinkle with vinegar.

scalloped potatoes with gorgonzola

scalloped potatoes with gorgonzola

Makes 8 servings

1 (14½-ounce) can chicken broth
1½ cups whipping cream
4 teaspoons minced garlic
1½ teaspoons dried sage leaves
1 cup BELGIOIOSO® Gorgonzola
   Cheese
2¼ pounds russet potatoes, peeled,
   halved and thinly sliced
Salt and pepper to taste

Preheat oven to 375°F. In medium heavy saucepan, simmer chicken broth, whipping cream, garlic and sage 5 minutes or until slightly thickened. Add BelGioioso® Gorgonzola Cheese and stir until melted. Remove from heat.

Place potatoes in large bowl and season with salt and pepper. Arrange half of potatoes in 13×9×2-inch glass baking dish. Pour half of cream mixture over top of potatoes. Repeat layers with remaining potatoes and cream mixture. Bake until potatoes are tender, about 1¼ hours. Let stand 15 minutes before serving.

mozzarella zucchini skillet

Makes 7 servings

2 tablespoons vegetable oil
5 medium zucchini, sliced
(about 7½ cups)
1 medium onion, chopped
(about ½ cup)
¼ teaspoon garlic powder **or**
2 cloves garlic, minced
1½ cups PREGO® Traditional Italian
Sauce **or** PREGO® Organic
Tomato & Basil Italian Sauce
½ cup shredded mozzarella cheese
or Cheddar cheese

1. Heat the oil in a 12-inch skillet over medium-high heat. Add the zucchini, onion and garlic powder and cook until the vegetables are tender-crisp.

2. Stir the sauce into the skillet and heat through.

3. Sprinkle with the cheese. Cover and cook until the cheese melts.

honey parsnips

Makes 4 servings

4 to 5 parsnips
½ cup honey
½ cup water
1 tablespoon butter or margarine,
melted

Peel parsnips and boil in salted water until tender. Drain and cut into thick slices; place in baking dish. Combine honey, ½ cup water and butter; pour mixture over parsnips. Bake parsnips at 350°F 10 minutes. Turn parsnips over and bake 10 minutes more. Place under broiler to brown.

Favorite recipe from **National Honey Board**

curried cauliflower & cashews

Makes 8 servings

1 head cauliflower, broken into
florets (about 4 cups)
½ cup water
¾ cup toasted unsalted cashews
3 tablespoons butter, divided
2 tablespoons all-purpose flour
1 tablespoon curry powder
1¼ cups milk
Salt and black pepper
1 cup plain dry bread crumbs
1 jar mango chutney (optional)

1. Preheat oven to 350°F. Grease 2-quart casserole.

2. Combine cauliflower and water in large microwavable dish. Microwave on HIGH 4 minutes or until almost tender. Drain; transfer to prepared casserole. Add cashews; stir until blended.

3. Melt 2 tablespoons butter in medium saucepan over medium heat. Add flour and curry powder; cook and stir 2 minutes. Add milk; cook until mixture thickens slightly, whisking constantly. Season with salt and pepper.

4. Pour sauce over cauliflower mixture; stir to coat. Top with bread crumbs. Dot with remaining 1 tablespoon butter.

5. Bake 45 minutes or until lightly browned. Serve with chutney, if desired.

squash casserole

squash casserole

Makes 8 servings

3 cups PEPPERIDGE FARM® Cornbread Stuffing
¼ cup butter **or** margarine, melted
1 can (10¾ ounces) CAMPBELL'S® Condensed Cream of Chicken Soup (Regular **or** 98% Fat Free)
½ cup sour cream
2 small yellow squash, shredded
2 small zucchini, shredded
¼ cup shredded carrot
½ cup shredded Cheddar cheese

1. Stir the stuffing and butter in a large bowl. Reserve ½ **cup** of the stuffing mixture and spoon remaining into a 2-quart shallow baking dish.

2. Stir the soup, sour cream, yellow squash, zucchini, carrot and cheese in a medium bowl. Spread the mixture over the stuffing mixture and sprinkle with the reserved stuffing mixture.

3. Bake at 350°F. for 40 minutes or until hot.

Prep Time: 15 minutes
Cook Time: 40 minutes

spicy asian slaw

Makes 4 servings

3 tablespoons rice vinegar
2 tablespoons soy sauce
1 tablespoon dark sesame oil
¼ teaspoon red pepper flakes, crushed
4 cups (8 ounces) packaged coleslaw mix (shredded fresh cabbage & carrots)
½ cup SUN•MAID® Natural Raisins
⅓ cup green onions, thinly sliced
¼ cup peanuts or cashews, chopped (optional)

COMBINE vinegar, soy sauce, sesame oil and pepper flakes in large bowl. Mix well.

ADD coleslaw mix, raisins and green onions. Toss well.

CHILL at least 1 hour or up to 24 hours before serving. Sprinkle with peanuts, if desired.

Prep Time: 10 minutes

picante pinto beans with bacon

Makes 6 servings

1 cup PACE® Picante Sauce
¼ cup ketchup **or** barbecue sauce
¼ cup packed brown sugar
1 teaspoon ground cumin
2 cans (about 15 ounces **each**) pinto beans, rinsed and drained
4 slices bacon, cooked and crumbled
Sliced jalapeño pepper

Heat the picante sauce, ketchup, brown sugar, cumin, beans and bacon in a 2-quart saucepan over medium heat until the mixture is hot and bubbling. Garnish with the jalapeño pepper.

ham seasoned peas

Makes 4 servings

1 teaspoon olive oil
½ cup cooked lean ham, chopped
¼ cup chopped onion
2 cups (about 9 ounces) frozen peas
¼ cup chicken broth
⅛ to ¼ teaspoon dried oregano
⅛ teaspoon black pepper (optional)

1. Heat oil in medium saucepan over medium heat. Add ham and onion; cook and stir until onion is tender.

2. Stir in peas, broth, oregano and pepper, if desired. Bring to a boil. Reduce heat to low; cover and simmer 4 minutes or until peas are tender.

Prep Time: 5 minutes
Cook Time: 10 minutes

bacon roasted brussels sprouts

Makes 4 servings

1 pound Brussels sprouts
3 slices bacon, cut into ½-inch pieces
2 teaspoons brown sugar
Salt and black pepper

1. Preheat oven to 400°F. Trim ends from Brussels sprouts; cut in half lengthwise.

2. Combine Brussels sprouts, bacon and brown sugar in 13×9-inch glass baking dish.

3. Roast 25 to 30 minutes or until golden brown, stirring once. Season with salt and pepper.

creamy smashed red potatoes with cheese

Makes 15 servings

3 pounds unpeeled new red potatoes, cut into quarters
1 cup or more NESTLÉ® CARNATION® Evaporated Lowfat 2% Milk
2 tablespoons butter, cut into pieces
¾ cup grated Parmesan cheese blend
Salt and ground black pepper to taste

PLACE potatoes in large saucepan. Cover with water; bring to a boil. Cook over medium-high heat for 15 to 20 minutes or until potatoes are tender; drain.

RETURN potatoes to saucepan. Beat with hand-held mixer for a few seconds to break up. Add evaporated milk and butter; beat until milk and butter are mixed in (some lumps will still be present). Add additional evaporated milk if a smoother consistency is desired. Stir in cheese. Season with salt and pepper to taste.

ham seasoned peas

braised beets with cranberries

braised beets with cranberries

Makes 6 to 8 servings

2½ pounds beets, peeled and cut into sixths
1 cup cranberry juice
½ cup dried cranberries
2 tablespoons honey
2 tablespoons butter, cut into small pieces
2 tablespoons quick-cooking tapioca
½ teaspoon salt
⅓ cup crumbled blue cheese (optional)
   Orange peel, thinly sliced or grated (optional)

Slow Cooker Directions

1. Combine beets, cranberry juice, cranberries, honey, butter, tapioca and salt in slow cooker. Cover; cook on LOW 7 to 8 hours or until beets are tender.

2. Transfer beets to serving bowl. Pour half of cooking liquid over beets. Serve warm, at room temperature or chilled. Sprinkle with blue cheese and orange peel, if desired.

Tip: Beets and blue cheese are an excellent combination. Because beets have such an earthy, rich flavor, they need a powerhouse cheese to accompany them. Try one of the popular varieties of blue cheese such as Gorgonzola, Roquefort or Stilton. If you find blue cheese too pungent, try a milder goat cheese instead.

peas florentine style

Makes 5 servings

2 (10-ounce) packages frozen peas
¼ cup FILIPPO BERIO® Olive Oil
4 ounces Canadian bacon, cubed
1 garlic clove, minced
1 tablespoon chopped fresh Italian
    parsley
1 teaspoon sugar
    Salt

Place peas in large colander or strainer; run under hot water until slightly thawed. Drain well. In medium skillet, heat olive oil over medium heat until hot. Add bacon and garlic; cook and stir 2 to 3 minutes or until garlic turns golden. Add peas and parsley; cook and stir over high heat 5 to 7 minutes or until heated through. Drain well. Stir in sugar; season to taste with salt.

vegetables in cream sauce

Makes 6 servings

1 package (16 ounces) frozen
    broccoli, cauliflower and carrot
    blend
¼ pound (4 ounces) VELVEETA®
    2% Milk Pasteurized Prepared
    Cheese Product, cut into ½-inch
    cubes
4 ounces (½ of 8-ounce package)
    PHILADELPHIA® ⅓ Less Fat
    Cream Cheese, cubed

Microwave Directions
LAYER ingredients in microwavable 1½-quart casserole; cover.

MICROWAVE on HIGH 13 minutes or until vegetables are heated through, stirring after 7 minutes; stir.

garlicky mustard greens

Makes 4 servings

2 pounds mustard greens
1 teaspoon olive oil
1 cup chopped onion
2 cloves garlic, minced
¾ cup chopped red bell pepper
½ cup chicken broth
1 tablespoon cider vinegar
1 teaspoon sugar

1. Remove stems and any wilted leaves from greens. Stack several leaves; roll up jelly-roll style. Cut crosswise into 1-inch slices. Repeat with remaining greens.

2. Heat oil in large saucepan over medium heat. Add onion and garlic; cook and stir 5 minutes or until onion is tender. Stir in greens, bell pepper and broth. Reduce heat to low. Cover; cook 25 minutes or until greens are tender, stirring occasionally.

3. Combine vinegar and sugar in small cup; stir until sugar is dissolved. Stir into cooked greens. Serve immediately.

garlicky mustard greens

sweet potato-cranberry bake

sweet potato-cranberry bake

Makes 4 to 6 servings

1 can (40 ounces) whole sweet
　potatoes, drained
1⅓ cups *French's*® French Fried
　Onions, divided
2 cups fresh cranberries
2 tablespoons packed brown sugar
⅓ cup honey

1. Preheat oven to 400°F. In 1½-quart
casserole, layer sweet potatoes,
⅔ cup French Fried Onions and *1 cup*
cranberries. Sprinkle with brown sugar;
drizzle with *half* the honey. Top with
remaining cranberries and honey.

2. Bake, covered, at 400°F for
35 minutes or until heated through.
Gently stir casserole. Top with
remaining ⅔ cup onions; bake,
uncovered, 1 to 3 minutes or until
onions are golden brown.

toasted corn & sage harvest risotto

Makes 6 servings

1 tablespoon olive oil
1 cup fresh **or** drained canned whole
　kernel corn
1 large orange **or** red pepper,
　chopped (about 1 cup)
1 medium onion, chopped (about
　½ cup)
1¾ cups **uncooked** regular long grain
　white rice
4 cups SWANSON® Chicken Broth
　(Regular, Natural Goodness® **or**
　Certified Organic)
1 teaspoon ground sage
1 can (10¾ ounces) CAMPBELL'S®
　Condensed Cream of Celery
　Soup (Regular **or** 98% Fat Free)
¼ cup grated Parmesan cheese

1. Heat the oil in a 4-quart saucepan
over medium heat. Add the corn,
pepper and onion and cook for
5 minutes or until the vegetables are
lightly browned.

2. Add the rice to the saucepan and
cook and stir for 30 seconds. Stir in
the broth and sage and heat to a boil.
Reduce the heat to low. Cover and
cook for 20 minutes or until the rice
is tender.

3. Stir in the soup. Cook for 2 minutes
or until the rice mixture is hot. Sprinkle
with the cheese.

Prep Time: 15 minutes
Cook Time: 35 minutes

southern spicy grilled corn

Makes 4 servings

½ cup HELLMANN'S® or BEST FOODS® Real Mayonnaise
2 tablespoons chopped onion
1 tablespoon apple cider vinegar
½ tablespoon finely chopped garlic
½ teaspoon chipotle powder
4 ears corn-on-the-cob, halved

1. In small bowl, combine all ingredients except corn.

2. Grill corn, brushing frequently with mayonnaise mixture, until corn is tender. Garnish, if desired, with chopped fresh cilantro or parsley.

green bean and onion casserole

Makes 6 servings

1 jar (1 pound) RAGÚ® Cheesy! Classic Alfredo Sauce
2 packages (9 ounces each) frozen green beans, thawed
1 can (2.8 ounces) French fried onions, divided
¼ teaspoon ground white pepper
1 tablespoon grated Parmesan cheese (optional)

1. Preheat oven to 350°F. In 1½-quart casserole, combine Alfredo Sauce, green beans, ½ of onions and pepper; sprinkle with cheese.

2. Bake, uncovered, 25 minutes or until hot and bubbling. Top with remaining onions and bake an additional 5 minutes.

Prep Time: 5 minutes
Cook Time: 30 minutes

garden vegetable rice medley

Makes 4 servings

1 cup water
1½ cups DOLE® Mini Cut Carrots
1 cup DOLE® Broccoli or Cauliflower florets
1 cup DOLE® Sugar Peas or Green Beans
2 medium red, yellow or green bell peppers, cut into 2-inch pieces
1 package (8 ounces) mushrooms, stems trimmed
3 cups hot cooked brown or white rice
1 cup (4 ounces) shredded low-fat Cheddar cheese
⅓ cup crumbled feta cheese

• Pour water in large saucepan; heat to boiling. Add carrots and broccoli. Reduce heat to low; cover and cook 5 minutes. Add sugar peas, bell peppers and mushrooms; cook 5 minutes more until vegetables are tender-crisp. Drain vegetables.

• Spoon hot rice onto large serving platter; top with vegetables and cheeses.

• Cover with aluminum foil; let stand 3 minutes or until cheeses melt.

southern spicy grilled corn

cauliflower gratin

Makes 6 servings

Vegetable cooking spray
1 can (10¾ ounces) CAMPBELL'S®
   Condensed Cream of Mushroom
   Soup (Regular **or** 98% Fat Free)
½ cup milk
1 clove garlic, minced
1 bag (20 ounces) frozen cauliflower
   flowerets, thawed (about 5 cups)
1 cup finely grated Swiss cheese
   (about 4 ounces)
¼ cup cooked crumbled bacon **or**
   real bacon bits

1. Spray an 11×8-inch shallow baking dish with cooking spray. Stir the soup, milk, garlic, cauliflower and ½ **cup** of the cheese in the casserole. Sprinkle with the bacon and remaining cheese.

2. Bake at 350°F. for 50 minutes or until the cauliflower is tender and mixture is hot and bubbly.

Prep Time: 10 minutes
Bake Time: 50 minutes

brown rice and shiitake pilaf

Makes 6 servings

1 tablespoon olive oil
1 cup (about 2 ounces) sliced shiitake
   mushrooms
1 cup asparagus spears, cut into
   1-inch pieces
1 clove garlic, minced
3 cups cooked brown rice
¼ cup pine nuts, toasted*
¼ cup sliced green onions
1 tablespoon grated lemon peel
½ teaspoon salt
½ teaspoon ground black pepper

*To toast pine nuts, place on baking sheet. Bake at 350°F 5 to 7 minutes or until lightly browned.

Heat oil in large skillet over medium-high heat. Add mushrooms, asparagus and garlic; cook and stir 1 to 2 minutes or until tender. Add rice, pine nuts, onions, lemon peel, salt and pepper. Stir until well blended; heat thoroughly.

Favorite recipe from **USA Rice**

cheddar spoonbread

Makes 6 servings

1½ cups water
¾ cup CREAM OF WHEAT® Cereal
   (1-minute, 2½-minute or
   10-minute stovetop cooking)
1 cup shredded reduced-fat Cheddar
   cheese
½ cup milk
3 eggs, separated
¼ teaspoon ground black pepper

1. In large saucepan, over high heat, heat water to a boil; slowly sprinkle in cereal, stirring constantly. Return mixture to a boil; reduce heat. Cook and stir until thickened, about 2 to 3 minutes. Remove from heat; stir in cheese until melted, then milk, egg yolks and pepper.

2. In small bowl, with electric mixer at high speed, beat egg whites until stiff peaks form; gently fold egg whites into cheese mixture. Pour into greased 8×8×2-inch baking dish. Bake at 375°F for 30 to 35 minutes or until set and browned. Serve immediately.

home-style corn cakes

cheesy mashed potatoes and turnips

Makes 8 servings

2 pounds all-purpose potatoes, peeled
1 pound turnips, peeled
¼ cup milk
½ cup shredded Cheddar cheese
¼ cup butter or margarine
1 teaspoon Original TABASCO® brand Pepper Sauce
½ teaspoon salt

In large saucepan over high heat, combine potatoes and turnips with enough water to cover. Bring to a boil and reduce heat to low; cover and simmer 25 to 30 minutes or until vegetables are tender. Drain. Return vegetables to saucepan; heat over high heat for a few seconds to eliminate any excess moisture, shaking saucepan to prevent sticking.

In small saucepan over medium heat, bring milk to a simmer. In large bowl, mash vegetables. Stir in warmed milk, cheese, butter, TABASCO® Sauce and salt.

home-style corn cakes

Makes about 18 corn cakes

1 cup yellow cornmeal
½ cup all-purpose flour
½ teaspoon baking powder
½ teaspoon baking soda
1 envelope LIPTON® RECIPE SECRETS® Onion Soup Mix*
¾ cup buttermilk
1 egg, beaten
1 can (14¾ ounces) cream-style corn
2 ounces roasted red peppers, chopped (about ¼ cup)
I CAN'T BELIEVE IT'S NOT BUTTER!® Spread

*Also terrific with LIPTON® RECIPE SECRETS® Golden Onion Soup Mix.

1. In large bowl, combine cornmeal, flour, baking powder and baking soda. In small bowl, blend soup mix with buttermilk, egg, corn and roasted red peppers; stir into cornmeal mixture.

2. In 12-inch nonstick skillet or on griddle, melt ½ teaspoon I Can't Believe It's Not Butter!® Spread over medium heat. Drop ¼ cup batter for each corn cake and cook, turning once, 5 minutes or until cooked through and golden brown. Remove to serving platter and keep warm. Repeat with remaining batter and additional I Can't Believe It's Not Butter!® Spread if needed. Serve, if desired, with sour cream and prepared salsa.

Tip: Leftover corn cakes can be wrapped and frozen. Remove them from the wrapping and reheat them straight from the freezer in a preheated 350°F oven for about 15 minutes.

chipotle cheddar polenta

Makes 4 servings

2 cups milk
1½ cups water
2 teaspoons minced garlic
2 teaspoons fresh thyme leaves, chopped
1 bay leaf
1½ teaspoons salt
½ teaspoon ground black pepper
1 cup polenta or cornmeal
4 tablespoons unsalted butter
½ cup (2 ounces) SARGENTO® BISTRO® Blends Shredded Chipotle Cheddar Cheese
2 tablespoons SARGENTO® ARTISAN BLENDS™ Shredded Parmesan Cheese

COMBINE milk, water, garlic, thyme, bay leaf, salt and pepper in a large, heavy saucepan. Bring to a boil and slowly add the polenta, whisking constantly.

REDUCE the heat to low and simmer, stirring often with a large wooden spoon, until the polenta thickens, about 5 minutes.

ADD butter and stir until melted. Add the cheeses and stir well. Serve hot.

Tip: Polenta is a staple in Northern Italian cuisine. It is prepared by cooking cornmeal and water together to a thick consistency. When it cools, polenta becomes firm and can then be cut into pieces and fried, broiled or baked. Polenta is most often served as a first course or side dish, but it can also be served for breakfast, similar to grits.

lemony cabbage slaw with curry

Makes 6 servings

4 cups shredded green or white cabbage
2 tablespoons chopped green bell pepper
2 tablespoons chopped red bell pepper
1 green onion, thinly sliced
2 tablespoons cider vinegar
1 tablespoon sugar
1 tablespoon lemon juice
1 teaspoon curry powder
½ teaspoon salt
½ teaspoon celery seeds

1. Mix cabbage, bell peppers and green onion in large bowl. Combine vinegar, sugar, lemon juice, curry powder, salt and celery seeds in small bowl. Pour over cabbage mixture; mix well.

2. Cover and refrigerate at least 4 hours or overnight, stirring occasionally.

lemony cabbage slaw with curry

vegetable gratin

Makes 6 to 8 servings

2 tablespoons olive oil
3 small *or* 1 large zucchini, cut into
   ¼-inch slices
⅛ teaspoon salt, divided
⅛ teaspoon thyme, divided
⅛ teaspoon rosemary, divided
⅛ teaspoon freshly ground black
   pepper, divided
1 (6.5-ounce) package ALOUETTE®
   Savory Vegetable Spreadable
   Cheese
2 cups fresh broccoli florets
2 small yellow squash, sliced
1 small onion, sliced
1 cup crushed wheat crackers

• Preheat oven to 350°F. Place oil in medium-sized gratin or shallow baking dish.

• Layer zucchini in prepared dish.

• Sprinkle zucchini lightly with half each of salt, thyme, rosemary and pepper.

• Place 3 tablespoons Alouette® on top of zucchini.

• Layer with broccoli, yellow squash, onion, remaining seasonings and Alouette® until dish is filled.

• Sprinkle with cracker crumbs; cover with foil. Bake 20 minutes.

• Remove foil; bake another 20 minutes. Brown lightly under broiler 1 to 2 minutes. Serve hot or at room temperature.

garlic fries

Makes 4 servings

1 bag (32 ounces) frozen French
   fried potatoes
1 envelope LIPTON® RECIPE
   SECRETS® Savory Herb with
   Garlic Soup Mix*

*Also terrific with LIPTON® RECIPE SECRETS®
Onion Soup Mix.*

1. Preheat oven to 450°F. In large bowl, thoroughly toss frozen French fried potatoes with soup mix; spread on jelly-roll pan.

2. Bake until golden and crisp, about 25 minutes, stirring once.

Prep Time: 5 minutes
Cook Time: 25 minutes

spinach pie

Makes 6 servings

1 tablespoon FILIPPO BERIO®
   Olive Oil
1 pound fresh spinach, washed,
   drained and stems removed
1 medium potato, cooked and
   mashed
2 eggs, beaten
¼ cup cottage cheese
2 tablespoons grated Romano
   cheese
   Salt

Preheat oven to 350°F. Grease 8-inch round cake pan with olive oil. Tear spinach into bite-size pieces. In large bowl, combine spinach, potato, eggs, cottage cheese and Romano cheese. Spoon mixture into prepared pan. Bake 15 to 20 minutes or until set. Season to taste with salt.

bayou dirty rice

Makes 4 to 6 servings

¼ pound spicy sausage, crumbled
½ medium onion, chopped
1 stalk celery, sliced
1 package (6 ounces) wild and long
 grain rice seasoned mix
1 can (14½ ounces) DEL MONTE®
 Original Recipe Stewed
 Tomatoes
½ green bell pepper, chopped
¼ cup chopped fresh parsley

1. Brown sausage and onion in large skillet over medium-high heat; drain. Add celery, rice and rice seasoning packet; cook and stir 2 minutes.

2. Drain tomatoes, reserving liquid; pour liquid into measuring cup. Add water to measure 1⅓ cups; pour over rice. Add tomatoes; bring to a boil. Cover and cook over low heat 20 minutes. Add bell pepper and parsley.

3. Cover and cook 5 minutes or until rice is tender.

bayou dirty rice

parmesan chive potato bake

Makes 8 servings

1½ pounds red bliss or thin skin
 potatoes
 1 cup HELLMANN'S® or BEST
 FOODS® Light Mayonnaise
½ cup milk
 8 tablespoons grated Parmesan
 cheese, divided
¼ cup chopped chives (optional)
½ teaspoon cracked black pepper

1. Preheat oven to 350°F.

2. Cover potatoes with cold water and bring to a boil over high heat in 3-quart saucepan. Reduce heat to low and simmer, uncovered, 15 minutes or until potatoes are fork-tender. Drain and cool.

3. Thinly slice potatoes and arrange in 13×9-inch baking dish; set aside.

4. Combine HELLMANN'S® or BEST FOODS® Light Mayonnaise, milk, 6 tablespoons cheese, chives and pepper in medium bowl. Evenly spoon mixture over potatoes. Top with remaining 2 tablespoons cheese.

5. Bake 25 minutes or until golden brown and bubbling.

Variation: Also terrific with HELLMANN'S® or BEST FOODS® Real Mayonnaise.

Prep Time: 10 minutes
Cook Time: 45 minutes

original green bean casserole

Makes 6 servings

1 can (10¾ ounces) condensed cream
   of mushroom soup, undiluted
¾ cup milk
⅛ teaspoon black pepper
2 packages (9 ounces each) frozen
   cut green beans, thawed*
1⅓ cups **French's**® French Fried
   Onions, divided

*Substitute 2 cans (14½ ounces each) cut green
beans, drained, for frozen green beans.

1. Preheat oven to 350°F. Combine
soup, milk and pepper in 1½-quart
casserole; stir until well blended. Stir in
beans and ⅔ *cup* French Fried Onions.

2. Bake, uncovered, 30 minutes or until
hot; stir. Sprinkle with remaining ⅔ *cup*
onions. Bake 5 minutes or until onions
are golden brown.

Microwave Directions: Prepare green
bean mixture as above in 1½-quart
microwave-safe casserole. Cover with
vented plastic wrap. Microwave on
HIGH 8 to 10 minutes or until heated
through, stirring halfway through
cooking time. Uncover. Top with
remaining onions. Cook 1 minute until
onions are golden. Let stand 5 minutes.

Prep Time: 5 minutes
Cook Time: 35 minutes

Tip: If you would like to use fresh
green beans in this recipe, choose
ones that are thin, crisp and brightly
colored. Keep them wrapped in the
refrigerator for up to 5 days. Before
adding them to the casserole, cut
them into bite-size pieces.

*roasted asparagus with chavrie®-dijon
sauce*

roasted asparagus with chavrie®-dijon sauce

Makes 6 servings

1½ pounds fresh asparagus spears,
   trimmed, cleaned
2 teaspoons extra virgin olive oil
1 package (5.3 ounces) CHAVRIE®
   goat cheese, plain
1 tablespoon whipping cream
1 teaspoon Dijon mustard
2 tablespoons capers, drained

Blanch asparagus for 1½ minutes. Heat
oven to 400°F. Arrange asparagus in
single layer in shallow baking pan.
Drizzle with olive oil. Bake 5 minutes
or until desired doneness.

In small microwavable bowl, mix
Chavrie®, cream and mustard.
Microwave on HIGH 30 seconds. Stir;
microwave another 30 seconds or until
warm. Stir in capers. Serve sauce with
asparagus.

southwest spaghetti squash

Makes 4 servings

1 spaghetti squash (about 3 pounds)
1 can (about 14 ounces) Mexican-style diced tomatoes
1 can (about 14 ounces) black beans, rinsed and drained
¾ cup (3 ounces) shredded Monterey Jack cheese, divided
¼ cup finely chopped fresh cilantro
1 teaspoon ground cumin
¼ teaspoon garlic salt
¼ teaspoon black pepper

1. Preheat oven to 350°F. Spray baking sheet and 1½-quart baking dish with nonstick cooking spray. Cut squash in half lengthwise. Remove and discard seeds. Place squash, cut side down, on prepared baking sheet. Bake 45 minutes or just until tender. Shred hot squash with fork; place in large bowl. (Use oven mitts to protect hands.)

2. Add tomatoes, beans, ½ cup cheese, cilantro, cumin, garlic salt and pepper; toss well. Spoon mixture into prepared baking dish. Sprinkle with remaining ¼ cup cheese.

3. Bake 30 to 35 minutes or until heated through. Serve immediately.

Tip: Spaghetti squash, a large oblong winter squash, has creamy yellow skin and pale yellow flesh. It gets its name because the flesh separates into spaghetti-like strands when cooked. The squash itself is somewhat bland, so it is a good base for flavorful sauces and additions like herbs and spices.

oat-topped sweet potato crisp

Makes 8 servings

1 package (8 ounces) PHILADELPHIA® Cream Cheese, softened
1 can (40 ounces) cut sweet potatoes, drained
¾ cup firmly packed brown sugar, divided
¼ teaspoon ground cinnamon
1 cup chopped apples
⅔ cup chopped cranberries
½ cup flour
½ cup old-fashioned or quick-cooking oats, uncooked
⅓ cup cold butter or margarine
¼ cup chopped PLANTERS® Pecans

PREHEAT oven to 350°F. Beat cream cheese, sweet potatoes, ¼ cup of the sugar and cinnamon with electric mixer on medium speed until well blended. Spoon into 1½-quart casserole dish; top with apples and cranberries.

MIX flour, oats and remaining ½ cup sugar in medium bowl; cut in butter until mixture resembles coarse crumbs. Stir in pecans. Sprinkle over fruit mixture.

BAKE 35 to 40 minutes or until heated through.

Prep Time: 20 minutes
Bake Time: 35 to 40 minutes

creamy spinach-stuffed portobellos

creamy spinach-stuffed portobellos

Makes 4 servings

1 tablespoon vegetable oil
1 medium onion, chopped
   (about ½ cup)
1 medium tomato, chopped
   (about 1 cup)
1 bag (about 6 ounces) fresh baby
   spinach leaves
1 can (10¾ ounces) CAMPBELL'S®
   Condensed Cream of Celery
   Soup (Regular **or** 98% Fat Free)
1 tablespoon bread crumbs, toasted
2 tablespoons grated Parmesan
   cheese
4 large portobello mushrooms,
   stems removed

1. Heat the oil in a 10-inch nonstick skillet over medium heat. Add the onion and cook until tender-crisp, stirring occasionally. Add the tomatoes and spinach and cook just until the spinach is wilted. Stir in the soup and cook until the mixture is hot and bubbling.

2. Stir the bread crumbs and cheese in a small bowl.

3. Place the mushroom caps onto a baking sheet. Spoon the spinach mixture into the mushroom caps.

4. Roast at 425°F. for 15 minutes or until the mushroom caps are tender. Remove the baking sheet from the oven. Sprinkle with the bread crumb mixture.

5. Heat the broiler. Broil the mushroom caps 4 inches from the heat until the topping is golden brown.

harvest rice

Makes 6 servings

1 tablespoon vegetable oil
1 cup julienne carrots
1 cup sliced green onions
2 cups cored and chopped unpeeled
   apples
3 cups cooked brown rice
½ cup seedless raisins
1 tablespoon sesame seeds
½ teaspoon salt

Heat oil in large skillet over medium-high heat. Cook carrots 3 to 5 minutes or until tender-crisp. Add onions and apples; cook 3 to 5 minutes. Stir in rice, raisins, sesame seeds and salt. Cook, stirring, 1 to 2 minutes or until heated thoroughly.

Favorite recipe from **USA Rice**

Tip: This is the perfect dish to prepare for an autumn meal, when apples and carrots are in season. Try it as a nontraditional side with your Thanksgiving turkey.

spicy skillet vegetables, salsa-style

Makes 8 servings

2 cups finely diced peeled potatoes
½ cup water
2 tablespoons vegetable oil
1 green bell pepper, cut into strips
1 red bell pepper, cut into strips
1 jar (16 ounces) ORTEGA® Salsa, any variety
1 can (15 ounces) ORTEGA® Black Beans, rinsed, drained
1 can (15 ounces) corn, drained
⅓ cup ORTEGA® Diced Jalapeños
1 cup (4 ounces) crumbled queso fresco or shredded Monterey Jack cheese

MICROWAVE potatoes with water, covered, on HIGH (100%) 5 minutes. Drain. Meanwhile, in large skillet, heat oil over medium-high heat.

COOK and stir bell pepper strips in skillet for 3 to 4 minutes. Stir in drained potatoes and salsa, then beans, corn and jalapeños.

BRING to a boil. Cover; reduce heat to medium and cook for 5 minutes, or until potatoes are tender.

SPRINKLE with cheese before serving.

Tip: If jalapeños are too hot for your family, use diced green chiles instead.

twice-baked potatoes with sun-dried tomatoes

Makes 8 servings

4 large baking potatoes
    Vegetable oil
1 container (16 ounces) sour cream
2 cups (8 ounces) shredded Cheddar cheese, divided
⅓ cup sun-dried tomatoes packed in oil, drained and chopped
4 tablespoons finely chopped green onions, divided
2 tablespoons butter, softened
1 teaspoon salt
½ teaspoon black pepper

1. Preheat oven to 350°F. Rub potatoes with oil; pierce in several places with fork. Bake 1 hour. Cool 30 minutes.

2. Cut potatoes in half lengthwise. Scrape potato pulp into large bowl, leaving ½-inch-thick shells. Add sour cream, 1½ cups cheese, sun-dried tomatoes, 3 tablespoons green onions, butter, salt and pepper; mix gently. Spoon into potato shells.

3. Place potatoes on baking sheet. Bake 15 to 20 minutes or until heated through. Top with remaining ½ cup cheese; bake 5 minutes or until cheese is melted. Sprinkle with remaining 1 tablespoon green onions.

spicy skillet vegetables, salsa-style

apple walnut dressing

Makes 4 servings

1 bag SUCCESS® Brown Rice
1 tart green apple, cored and
  chopped
2 tablespoons lemon juice
1 teaspoon apple pie spice
  Vegetable cooking spray
4 ounces bulk turkey sausage
¾ cup chopped onion
½ cup chopped celery
¼ cup chopped walnuts
¼ cup raisins
½ teaspoon salt
½ teaspoon pepper
⅛ teaspoon dried sage
⅓ cup low-sodium chicken broth
¼ cup honey

Prepare rice as directed on package.

Combine apples, lemon juice and spice
in large bowl; mix lightly. Set aside.
Spray large skillet with cooking spray.
Crumble sausage into prepared skillet.
Cook over medium heat until browned,
stirring occasionally.

Add onion, celery, walnuts and raisins;
cook until crisp-tender. Add apple
mixture and seasonings; cook and stir
3 minutes. Add rice, broth and honey;
heat thoroughly, stirring consistently.

new potatoes in dill cream sauce

new potatoes in dill cream sauce

Makes 16 servings

2½ pounds new red potatoes,
  quartered
1 tub (8 ounces) PHILADELPHIA®
  Chive & Onion Cream Cheese
  Spread
¼ cup milk
1 green pepper, chopped
3 tablespoons chopped fresh dill

PLACE potatoes in large saucepan. Add
enough water to cover potatoes. Bring
to boil on medium-high heat. Reduce
heat to medium; simmer 15 minutes or
until potatoes are tender. Drain.

MIX cream cheese spread, milk and
green pepper in large microwavable
bowl. Microwave on HIGH 40 to
50 seconds or until cream cheese spread
is melted; stir until well blended. Stir
in dill.

ADD potatoes; toss to coat.

lemon brussels sprouts

Makes 4 servings

1 package (10 ounces) frozen
  Brussels sprouts
1 tablespoon water
¼ teaspoon grated lemon peel
½ teaspoon lemon juice
  Black pepper
  Ground thyme

Microwave Directions
1. Combine Brussels sprouts, water,
lemon peel and lemon juice in
1-quart microwavable casserole. Cover;
microwave on HIGH 3 minutes.

2. Stir. Cover; microwave 2 to 3 minutes
or until Brussels sprouts are tender.
Drain; season with pepper and thyme.

main dishes

main dishes

· · · · ·

family-favorite roast chicken

Makes 8 servings

- 1 (4½-pound) roasting chicken
- ¼ teaspoon black pepper
- ⅛ teaspoon salt
- 1 medium lemon, washed
- 4 ounces (½ of 8-ounce package) PHILADELPHIA® Cream Cheese, softened
- 1 tablespoon Italian seasoning
- ½ cup KRAFT® Zesty Italian Dressing

PREHEAT oven to 350°F. Rinse chicken; pat dry with paper towel. Use the tip of a sharp knife to separate the chicken skin from the meat in the chicken breast and tops of the legs. Sprinkle chicken both inside and out with the pepper and salt. Place in 13×9-inch baking dish.

GRATE the lemon; mix the peel with cream cheese and Italian seasoning. Use a small spoon or your fingers to carefully stuff the cream cheese mixture under the chicken skin, pushing the cream cheese mixture carefully toward the legs, being careful to not tear the skin.

CUT the lemon in half; squeeze both halves into small bowl. Add dressing; beat with wire whisk until well blended. Drizzle evenly over chicken. Place the squeezed lemon halves inside the chicken cavity. Insert an ovenproof meat thermometer into thickest part of one of the chicken's thighs.

BAKE 1 hour 30 minutes or until chicken is no longer pink in center (165°F), basting occasionally with the pan juices.

Tip: To get the most juice from a lemon, let it come to room temperature then roll it around on the countertop before cutting, pressing down with the palm of your hand.

oven-fried chicken tenders

Makes 4 servings

¾ cup vegetable oil
1 cup buttermilk
1 egg, beaten
1 cup all-purpose flour
2 to 3 teaspoons Cajun seasoning
¾ teaspoon paprika
½ teaspoon garlic powder
1½ pounds chicken tenders
   Salt and black pepper

1. Place large roasting pan on rack of cold oven; add oil. Heat oven to 425°F.

2. Meanwhile, whisk buttermilk and egg in medium bowl until well blended. Combine flour, seasoning, paprika and garlic powder in shallow dish. Dip chicken into flour mixture, then buttermilk mixture, then again into flour mixture. Place on plate in single layer. (If flour coating becomes moist, coat with flour mixture again.)

3. Place chicken in roasting pan in oven. Bake 6 minutes. Turn; bake 6 minutes or until golden brown and no longer pink in center. Season with salt and pepper.

oven-fried chicken tenders

deliciously italian rigatoni

Makes 8 servings

8 ounces uncooked rigatoni pasta
1 pound ground beef
1 can (8 ounces) tomato sauce
1 can (6 ounces) tomato paste
½ cup water
3 cloves minced garlic
1 teaspoon onion salt
1 teaspoon Italian seasoning
1 teaspoon cayenne pepper, divided
¾ teaspoon sugar
2 tablespoons olive oil
2 tablespoons flour
2½ cups milk
1½ cups Italian blend of 6 cheeses or any combination of mozzarella, smoked provolone, Parmesan, Romano, fontina and Asiago
½ cup freshly grated Parmesan cheese
   Fresh parsley, chopped

Cook pasta according to package directions; drain.

In a large skillet over medium heat, brown ground beef; drain. Add tomato sauce, tomato paste, water, garlic, onion salt, Italian seasoning, ¾ teaspoon cayenne pepper and sugar; heat through.

In a saucepan, mix oil with flour and ¼ teaspoon cayenne pepper; add milk. Bring to a boil, whisking until smooth. Add Italian blend cheese and whisk until smooth. Pour cheese sauce over drained pasta. Pour into 13×9-inch baking pan coated with nonstick cooking spray. Spread tomato sauce mixture over pasta. Sprinkle with Parmesan cheese and parsley. Bake in a preheated 350°F oven for 30 minutes.

Favorite recipe from **North Dakota Wheat Commission**

chicken, hummus and vegetable wraps

Makes 4 servings

¾ cup hummus (regular, roasted red pepper or roasted garlic)
4 (8- to 10-inch) sun-dried tomato wraps or whole wheat tortillas
2 cups chopped cooked chicken
    Chipotle hot pepper sauce or Louisiana-style hot pepper sauce
½ cup shredded carrots
½ cup chopped unpeeled cucumber
½ cup thinly sliced radishes
2 tablespoons chopped fresh mint

Spread hummus evenly over wraps all the way to edges. Arrange chicken over hummus; sprinkle with hot pepper sauce. Top with carrots, cucumber, radishes and mint. Roll up tightly. Cut in half diagonally.

slow cooker turkey and dressing

Makes 4 servings

1 pound BOB EVANS® Sage or Original Recipe Sausage Roll
1 package (6 ounces) herb seasoned cubed stuffing
2 cups chicken broth, divided
½ cup dried cranberries
2 sweet potatoes, peeled and cut into 2-inch pieces
1 pound turkey breast cutlets

Slow Cooker Directions
In large skillet over medium heat, crumble and cook sausage until brown. Stir in stuffing, 1½ cups broth and cranberries; set aside. Place sweet potatoes in slow cooker. Place turkey on top. Add ½ cup broth. Pour sausage mixture over turkey. Cover and cook on LOW 4 to 6 hours.

chipotle-rubbed flank steak

chipotle-rubbed flank steak

Makes 4 to 6 servings

1 packet (1.25 ounces) ORTEGA® Smokey Chipotle Taco Seasoning Mix, divided
½ cup water
¼ cup REGINA® Red Wine Vinegar
1½ to 2 pounds flank steak
1 tablespoon olive oil
1 small onion, diced
1 tablespoon ORTEGA® Fire-Roasted Diced Green Chiles
1 cup ORTEGA® Garden Salsa
    Juice from ½ lime

COMBINE half of seasoning mix, water and vinegar in shallow dish. Add steak and turn to coat well. Marinate 15 minutes in refrigerator. Turn over and marinate 15 minutes longer.

HEAT oil in small saucepan over medium heat. Add onion; cook and stir 5 minutes or until translucent. Stir in chiles and salsa; cook and stir over low heat 5 minutes.

SPRINKLE remaining seasoning mix over both sides of steak. Broil or grill steak over high heat 5 minutes on each side, or to desired doneness. Let stand 5 minutes before slicing against grain. To serve, drizzle on sauce and lime juice.

linguine with herbs, tomatoes and capers

Makes 4 servings

- 1 package (9 ounces) refrigerated linguine
- 2 tablespoons olive oil
- 2 cloves garlic, minced
- 2 cups chopped tomatoes
- ¼ cup finely chopped green onions, green parts only
- 3 tablespoons capers, drained
- 2 tablespoons chopped fresh basil
- ¼ teaspoon salt
- ⅛ teaspoon black pepper
- ½ cup shredded Parmesan cheese

1. Cook linguine according to package directions; drain well.

2. Meanwhile, heat oil in large skillet over medium-high heat. Add garlic and tomatoes; cook 3 minutes or until tomatoes begin to soften, stirring frequently. Stir in green onions, capers and basil. Season with salt and pepper.

3. Add linguine to skillet; toss with tomato mixture. Sprinkle with cheese.

crispy onion tilapia fillets

Makes 4 servings

- 3 cups *French's*® French Fried Onions
- 1 tablespoon minced cilantro
- 1 teaspoon grated lime zest
- ½ teaspoon paprika
- ¼ cup flour
- 4 (½-inch thick) tilapia or red snapper fillets, split in half lengthwise if large
- 2 eggs, beaten

1. Place French Fried Onions, cilantro, lime zest and paprika in plastic bag. Crush onions with hands or rolling pin; shake to combine.

2. Place flour in another plastic bag. Add fillets; shake to coat. Dip fillets into egg, then into onion crumbs. Place on baking sheet.

3. Bake at 400°F for 15 minutes or until fish flakes easily with fork.

pepper and turkey stir-fry

Makes 4 servings

- 1 pound turkey cutlets or slices, cut into ¼-inch strips
- ½ teaspoon salt
- ¼ teaspoon black pepper
- 1 tablespoon olive oil, divided
- 1 red bell pepper, cut into ¼-inch strips
- 1 yellow bell pepper, cut into ¼-inch strips
- 1 pound fresh spinach, stems removed and coarsely chopped
- 2 tablespoons sugar
- 2 tablespoons balsamic vinegar

1. In medium bowl, combine turkey, salt and black pepper. In large nonstick skillet, over medium-high heat, sauté turkey in 2 teaspoons oil 4 to 5 minutes or until turkey is no longer pink in center. *Do not overcook.* Remove turkey from skillet; set aside.

2. Add remaining 1 teaspoon oil to skillet and sauté bell peppers 2 minutes. Gently fold in spinach.

3. In small bowl, combine sugar and vinegar; stir into vegetable mixture. Reduce heat to medium and stir-fry 2 to 3 minutes or until vegetables are tender. Return turkey strips to skillet and heat well. Serve immediately.

Favorite recipe from **National Turkey Federation**

linguine with herbs, tomatoes and capers

italian chicken breasts

italian chicken breasts

Makes 4 servings

  1 pound BOB EVANS® Italian Roll Sausage
  1 cup sliced fresh mushrooms
  1 clove garlic, minced
  3 (8-ounce) cans tomato sauce
  1 (6-ounce) can tomato paste
1½ teaspoons Italian seasoning
  4 boneless, skinless chicken breast halves
  1 cup (4 ounces) shredded mozzarella cheese
  Hot cooked pasta

Preheat oven to 350°F. Crumble sausage into large skillet. Cook over medium heat until browned, stirring occasionally. Remove sausage; set aside. Add mushrooms and garlic to drippings; cook and stir until tender. Stir in reserved sausage, tomato sauce, tomato paste and seasoning. Bring to a boil. Reduce heat to low; simmer 15 minutes to blend flavors. Meanwhile, arrange chicken in greased 11×7-inch baking dish. Pour tomato sauce mixture over chicken; cover with foil. Bake 40 minutes; uncover. Sprinkle with cheese; bake 5 minutes more. Serve over pasta. Refrigerate leftovers.

quick & crispy mac & cheese

Makes 4 to 6 servings

1⅓ cups (2.8 ounces) **French's®** Original or Cheddar French Fried Onions
  1 jar (15 ounces) Cheddar cheese sauce (microwave 1 minute to thin sauce)
  1 cup milk
  3 cups cooked tube-shaped pasta
  2 cups shredded Cheddar or cubed American cheese

1. Heat oven to 350°F. Lightly crush French Fried Onions in plastic bag using hands or rolling pin.

2. Mix cheese sauce and milk in greased 2-quart baking dish. Stir in pasta and 1 cup cheese.

3. Bake 25 minutes or until heated through. Stir. Top with remaining 1 cup cheese and onions. Bake 5 minutes or until golden.

tangy lemon pepper shrimp

Makes 2 to 3 servings

  1 carton (16 ounces) SEAPAK® Shrimp Scampi, frozen
 ½ cup dry white wine
  2 tablespoons Dijon mustard
  1 teaspoon lemon pepper

Heat large sauté skillet on medium for 1 minute. Add frozen shrimp to pan and sauté 6 minutes. Whisk wine, Dijon mustard and lemon pepper in a small bowl. Pour mixture over shrimp. Stir well to incorporate all ingredients. Simmer for additional 3 to 5 minutes (or until shrimp are fully cooked), stirring frequently. Serve shrimp over pasta or rice.

caribbean glazed swordfish with grilled pineapple chutney

Makes 4 servings

½ cup **Frank's® RedHot®** Cayenne Pepper Sauce or **Frank's® RedHot®** XTRA Hot Cayenne Pepper Sauce
¼ cup packed light brown sugar
1 teaspoon dried thyme leaves
½ teaspoon ground allspice
2 tablespoons olive oil
4 swordfish steaks, 1-inch thick, seasoned with salt and pepper
Grilled Pineapple Chutney (recipe follows)

1. Whisk together **Frank's Redhot** Sauce, sugar, thyme and allspice. Reserve 3 tablespoons mixture for Grilled Pineapple Chutney.

2. Mix oil into remaining hot sauce mixture; thoroughly baste fish.

3. Place fish on well-greased grill. Cook, covered, over medium-high direct heat for 10 to 15 minutes until opaque in center, turning once. Serve with Grilled Pineapple Chutney.

grilled pineapple chutney

½ of a fresh pineapple, peeled and sliced ½-inch thick
1 red or orange bell pepper, cut into quarters
2 tablespoons minced red onion
1 tablespoon minced candied ginger
1 tablespoon minced cilantro leaves

Grill pineapple and bell pepper about 10 minutes over medium direct heat until lightly charred and tender. Coarsely chop and place in bowl. Add reserved 3 tablespoons hot sauce mixture, onion, ginger and cilantro. Toss to combine.   *Makes 3 cups*

caribbean glazed swordfish with grilled pineapple chutney

smoked sausage and cabbage

Makes 4 servings

- 1 pound smoked sausage, cut into 2-inch pieces
- 1 tablespoon olive oil
- 6 cups coarsely chopped cabbage
- 1 yellow onion, cut into ½-inch wedges
- 2 cloves garlic, minced
- ¾ teaspoon sugar
- ¼ teaspoon caraway seeds
- ¼ teaspoon salt
- ¼ teaspoon black pepper
- 1 package (2 pounds) refrigerated mashed potatoes*

You may substitute thawed frozen mashed potatoes.

1. Heat large nonstick skillet over medium-high heat. Add sausage; cook and stir 3 minutes or until browned. Transfer to plate.

2. Heat oil in same skillet. Add cabbage, onion, garlic, sugar, caraway seeds, salt and pepper; cook and stir 5 minutes or until onion begins to brown. Add sausage; cover and cook 5 minutes. Remove from heat. Let stand 5 minutes.

3. Meanwhile, heat potatoes in microwave according to package directions. Serve sausage mixture over mashed potatoes.

Tip: To prepare fresh mashed potatoes, scrub 2 pounds potatoes and cut into pieces. Cover with water in large saucepan and bring to a boil. Simmer 15 minutes or until tender. Drain and mash potatoes, adding milk, sour cream or butter to make a smooth consistency. Season with salt and black pepper.

cashew chicken stir-fry

Makes 4 servings

- 2 tablespoons vegetable oil, divided
- 3 boneless, skinless chicken breasts (about 12 ounces), cut into ½-inch pieces
- ¼ cup reduced-sodium soy sauce, divided
- 2 cloves garlic, minced
- 1 teaspoon ground ginger
- 2 tablespoons cornstarch
- 3 cups broccoli florets
- 1 red bell pepper, diced
- 1½ cups chicken broth
- 1 tablespoon brown sugar, firmly packed
- 2 teaspoons sesame oil
- ½ cup FISHER® CHEF'S NATURALS® Dry Roasted Cashews
- Cooked Asian noodles or rice (optional)

1. In wok or large skillet, heat 1 tablespoon vegetable oil over medium-high heat 1 minute until hot. Add chicken, 2 tablespoons soy sauce, garlic and ginger; stir-fry 4 to 5 minutes until chicken is no longer pink. Transfer chicken to platter; loosely cover to keep warm.

2. Combine cornstarch and remaining 2 tablespoons soy sauce; set aside. Add remaining 1 tablespoon vegetable oil to wok. Add broccoli and red bell pepper; stir-fry 3 to 4 minutes.

3. Return chicken to wok; add chicken broth, brown sugar and sesame oil. Cook 2 to 3 minutes until broth begins to bubble. Stir in cornstarch mixture; reduce heat to medium. Cook 3 to 4 minutes until sauce thickens. Stir in cashews. Serve over cooked noodles or rice, if desired.

amazin' crab rice cakes

amazin' crab rice cakes

Makes 4 servings

1 cup chicken broth
1 cup MINUTE® White Rice, uncooked
2 eggs
2 cans (6 ounces each) crabmeat, drained, flaked*
2 tablespoons seafood seasoning
¼ cup (½ stick) butter or margarine
Fresh lemon wedges (optional)

*Or substitute 12 ounces canned salmon.

Bring broth to a boil in small saucepan. Stir in rice; cover. Remove from heat; let stand 5 minutes. Fluff with fork.

Beat eggs lightly in medium bowl. Add rice, crabmeat and seasoning; mix well. Refrigerate 5 minutes. Shape into 8 patties.

Melt butter in large skillet over medium heat. Add patties; cook 5 minutes on each side or until golden brown and heated through. Serve with lemon, if desired.

layered pasta casserole

Makes 6 to 8 servings

8 ounces uncooked penne pasta
8 ounces mild Italian sausage,
   casings removed
8 ounces ground beef
1 jar (about 26 ounces) pasta sauce
1 package (10 ounces) frozen
   chopped spinach, thawed and
   squeezed dry
2 cups (8 ounces) shredded
   mozzarella cheese, divided
1 cup whole milk ricotta cheese
½ cup grated Parmesan cheese
1 egg
2 tablespoons chopped fresh basil
   or 2 teaspoons dried basil
1 teaspoon salt

1. Preheat oven to 350°F. Spray
13×9-inch baking dish with nonstick
cooking spray. Cook pasta according to
package directions; drain. Transfer to
prepared dish.

2. Brown sausage and ground beef in
large skillet over medium-high heat
6 to 8 minutes, stirring to break up
meat; drain fat. Add pasta sauce; mix
well. Add half of meat sauce to pasta;
toss to coat.

3. Combine spinach, 1 cup mozzarella
cheese, ricotta cheese, Parmesan
cheese, egg, basil and salt in medium
bowl. Spoon small mounds of spinach
mixture over pasta mixture; spread
evenly with back of spoon. Top with
remaining meat sauce; sprinkle with
remaining 1 cup mozzarella cheese.
Bake 30 minutes.

pizza meat loaf

Makes 8 servings

1 envelope LIPTON® RECIPE
   SECRETS® Onion Soup Mix
2 pounds ground beef
1½ cups fresh bread crumbs
2 eggs
1 small green bell pepper, chopped
   (optional)
¼ cup water
1 cup RAGÚ® Old World Style®
   Pasta Sauce
1 cup shredded mozzarella cheese
   (about 4 ounces)

1. Preheat oven to 350°F. In large bowl,
combine all ingredients except ½ cup
Pasta Sauce and ½ cup cheese.

2. In 13×9-inch baking or roasting pan,
shape into loaf. Top with remaining
½ cup Pasta Sauce.

3. Bake, uncovered, 50 minutes. Sprinkle
top with remaining ½ cup cheese. Bake
an additional 10 minutes or until done.
Let stand 10 minutes before serving.

Prep Time: 10 minutes
Cook Time: 1 hour

layered pasta casserole

barbecued pork spareribs

Makes 4 servings

4 pounds pork spareribs, cut into
    serving-sized pieces
1 can (10¼ ounces) CAMPBELL'S®
    Beef Gravy
¾ cup barbecue sauce
2 tablespoons packed brown sugar

1. Place the ribs into an 8-quart
saucepot and add water to cover. Heat
over medium-high heat to a boil.
Reduce the heat to low. Cover and cook
for 30 minutes or until the meat is
tender. Drain the ribs well in a colander.

2. Stir the gravy, barbecue sauce and
brown sugar in a large bowl. Add the
ribs and toss to coat.

3. Lightly oil the grill rack and heat
the grill to medium-high. Grill the ribs
for 10 minutes, turning and brushing
occasionally with the gravy mixture,
until the ribs are well glazed.

pesto-topped halibut

Makes 4 servings

⅓ cup HELLMANN'S® or BEST
    FOODS® Mayonnaise Dressing
    with Extra Virgin Olive Oil
1 cup loosely packed fresh basil
    leaves
¼ cup pine nuts or walnuts
¼ cup grated Parmesan cheese
1 clove garlic
4 halibut or cod fillets
    (about 1 pound)

1. Preheat oven to 425°F. Lightly grease
baking sheet; set aside.

2. In food processor or blender, process
all ingredients except halibut until well
blended. Evenly spread on halibut.

3. Bake 15 minutes or until halibut
flakes with a fork.

ham with fruited bourbon sauce

Makes 10 to 12 servings

1 bone-in ham (about 6 pounds)
¾ cup packed dark brown sugar
½ cup raisins
½ cup apple juice
1 teaspoon ground cinnamon
¼ teaspoon red pepper flakes
⅓ cup dried cherries
¼ cup cornstarch
¼ cup bourbon, rum or apple juice

Slow Cooker Directions
1. Coat CROCK-POT® slow cooker
with nonstick cooking spray. Add ham,
cut side up. Combine brown sugar,
raisins, apple juice, cinnamon and
pepper flakes in small bowl; stir well.
Pour mixture evenly over ham. Cover;
cook on LOW 9 to 10 hours or on HIGH
4½ to 5 hours. Add cherries 30 minutes
before end of cooking time.

2. Transfer ham to cutting board. Let
stand 15 minutes before slicing.

3. Meanwhile, pour cooking liquid
into large measuring cup and let stand
5 minutes. Skim and discard excess fat.
Return cooking liquid to CROCK-POT®
slow cooker.

4. Turn CROCK-POT® slow cooker to
HIGH. Whisk cornstarch and bourbon
in small bowl until cornstarch is
dissolved. Stir into cooking liquid.
Cover; cook on HIGH 15 to 20 minutes
or until thickened. Serve sauce over
sliced ham.

barbecued pork spareribs

garlic & lemon herb marinated chicken

garlic & lemon herb marinated chicken

Makes 4 servings

3 to 4 pounds bone-in chicken
   pieces, skinned if desired
⅓ cup **French's®** Honey Dijon Mustard
⅓ cup lemon juice
⅓ cup olive oil
3 cloves garlic, minced
1 tablespoon grated lemon zest
1 tablespoon minced fresh thyme or
   rosemary
1 teaspoon coarse salt
½ teaspoon coarse black pepper

1. Place chicken into resealable plastic food storage bag. Combine remaining ingredients. Pour over chicken. Marinate in refrigerator 1 to 3 hours.

2. Remove chicken from marinade. Grill chicken over medium direct heat for 35 to 45 minutes until juices run clear near bone (170°F for breast meat; 180°F for dark meat). Serve with additional mustard on the side.

Prep Time: 10 minutes
Cook Time: 45 minutes
Marinate Time: 1 to 3 hours

hurry-up lasagna

Makes 10 servings

1 jar (48 ounces) tomato and sliced
   mushroom pasta sauce
2 packages (9 ounces each) fresh
   fettuccine, uncooked
4 cups (30 ounces) SARGENTO®
   Whole Milk Ricotta Cheese
1 cup minced fresh parsley
4 ounces thinly sliced pepperoni,
   divided
3 cups (12 ounces) SARGENTO®
   FANCY SHREDDED PIZZA
   DOUBLE CHEESE®, divided

SPREAD 1 cup sauce in bottom of 13×9-inch baking pan. Carefully place one-third uncooked fettuccine over sauce, making sure fettuccine is covered with sauce.

COMBINE Ricotta cheese and parsley. Layer 2 cups Ricotta mixture, half of the pepperoni, 1 cup sauce and 1 cup shredded cheese. Repeat layers of fettuccine, 2 cups Ricotta mixture, pepperoni, sauce and 1 cup shredded cheese. Top with remaining fettuccine and sauce, making sure sauce completely covers fettuccine.

COVER and bake in preheated 375°F oven 1 hour. Uncover; bake 5 minutes more. Sprinkle with remaining 1 cup shredded cheese. Let stand 10 minutes before serving.

Prep Time: 20 minutes
Cook Time: 65 minutes

Tip: This lasagna recipe substitutes fresh fettuccine for the standard lasagna sheets. Because fresh pasta is often made with eggs, this version will taste richer than a recipe using dry pasta. Also, the differently shaped pasta used here will give this dish a unique texture.

spaghetti bolognese

Makes 8 servings

6 slices bacon, cut into ½-inch pieces
1 large onion, diced (about 1 cup)
3 cloves garlic, minced
2 pounds ground beef
4 cups PREGO® Traditional Italian
    Sauce
1 cup milk
1 pound spaghetti, cooked and
    drained*
Grated Parmesan cheese

Reserve some of the cooking water from the spaghetti. You can use it to adjust the consistency of the finished sauce, if you like.

Slow Cooker Directions

1. Cook the bacon in a 12-inch skillet over medium-high heat until it's crisp. Remove the bacon from the skillet. Pour off all but **1 tablespoon** of the drippings.

2. Add the onion and cook in the hot drippings until tender. Add the garlic and beef and cook until the beef is well browned, stirring often. Pour off any fat.

3. Stir the bacon, beef mixture, Italian sauce and milk in a 6-quart slow cooker.

4. Cover and cook on HIGH for 4 to 5 hours.** Toss the spaghetti with the sauce. Sprinkle with the cheese, as desired.

***Or on LOW for 7 to 8 hours.*

Prep Time: 15 minutes
Cook Time: 4 to 5 hours

garlic-lemon shrimp with arugula

Makes 4 servings

2 tablespoons BERTOLLI® Olive Oil
1 pound medium shrimp
2 tablespoons white wine
2 tablespoons lemon juice, divided
1 envelope LIPTON® RECIPE
    SECRETS® Savory Herb with
    Garlic Soup Mix
1 cup water
4 cups loosely packed arugula or
    spinach leaves

1. In 12-inch nonstick skillet, heat oil over medium-high heat and cook shrimp, stirring occasionally, 3 minutes. Add wine and 1 tablespoon lemon juice and cook 2 minutes. Stir in soup mix blended with water and simmer 3 minutes.

2. Stir in arugula and cook 2 minutes or until just wilted but still green.

3. Remove shrimp mixture to serving platter and drizzle with remaining lemon juice. Serve, if desired, over hot cooked rice.

Prep Time: 10 minutes
Cook Time: 10 minutes

spaghetti bolognese

fish tacos

fish tacos

Makes 4 servings

REYNOLDS WRAP® Non-Stick Foil
4 tilapia fillets (4 to 6 ounces each)
    fresh or frozen, thawed
1 tablespoon fresh lime juice
1 teaspoon olive oil
1 teaspoon seafood seasoning
1 clove garlic, minced
½ teaspoon salt
⅛ teaspoon red pepper flakes
8 flour tortillas (8 inch)
    Lettuce, mango salsa and sliced
    avocado

Preheat oven to 400°F. For easy cleanup, line a 13×9-inch baking pan with Reynolds Wrap Non-Stick Foil with non-stick (dull) side toward food.

Place tilapia in foil-lined pan.

Mix lime juice, olive oil, seafood seasoning, garlic, salt and red pepper flakes in a medium bowl until well blended. Pour over fish.

Bake 15 to 20 minutes or until fish flakes easily with fork. Serve half of fillet in each tortilla with lettuce, mango salsa and avocado.

garlic pork kabobs

Makes 4 servings

1¾ cups SWANSON® Chicken Stock
2 tablespoons cornstarch
2 cloves garlic, minced
1 tablespoon packed brown sugar
1 tablespoon ketchup
2 teaspoons vinegar
1 boneless pork loin (about 1 pound),
    cut into 1-inch cubes
12 medium mushrooms
1 large red onion, cut into
    12 wedges
4 cherry tomatoes
4 cups hot cooked regular long grain
    white rice

1. Stir the stock, cornstarch, garlic, brown sugar, ketchup and vinegar in a 2-quart saucepan. Cook and stir over medium-high heat until the mixture boils and thickens. Remove the saucepan from the heat.

2. Thread alternately the pork, mushrooms and onion onto **4** skewers.

3. Lightly oil the grill rack and heat the grill to medium. Grill the kabobs for 20 minutes or until the pork is cooked through, turning and brushing often with the stock mixture. Place **1** tomato onto the end of each skewer.

4. Heat the remaining stock mixture over medium heat to a boil. Serve the stock mixture with the kabobs and rice.

Prep Time: 15 minutes
Cook Time: 25 minutes

baked bow tie pasta in mushroom cream sauce

Makes 6 servings

1 teaspoon olive oil
1 large onion, thinly sliced
1 package (10 ounces) sliced
    mushrooms
⅛ teaspoon ground black pepper
1 jar (1 pound) RAGÚ® Cheesy!®
    Light Parmesan Alfredo Sauce
8 ounces bow tie pasta, cooked and
    drained
1 tablespoon grated Parmesan
    cheese
1 tablespoon plain dry bread crumbs
    (optional)

1. Preheat oven to 400°F. In 10-inch nonstick skillet, heat oil over medium heat and cook onion, mushrooms and pepper, stirring frequently, 10 minutes or until vegetables are golden. Stir in Alfredo Sauce.

2. In 2-quart shallow baking dish, combine sauce mixture with hot pasta. Sprinkle with cheese combined with bread crumbs. Cover with aluminum foil and bake 20 minutes. Remove foil and bake an additional 5 minutes.

Prep Time: 10 minutes
Cook Time: 35 minutes

garlic pork kabobs

cheesy chimichangas

Makes 8 servings

1½ pounds lean ground beef
2 large onions, chopped
2 teaspoons garlic salt
½ teaspoon black pepper
8 (8-inch) ORTEGA® Soft Flour Tortillas
2 tablespoons vegetable oil, divided
1 jar (16 ounces) ORTEGA® Salsa, any variety, divided
2 cups (8 ounces) shredded Cheddar cheese, divided
2 cups (8 ounces) shredded Monterey Jack cheese, divided
   Shredded lettuce
   Chopped tomatoes
1 jar (11.5 ounces) ORTEGA® Guacamole Style Dip

PREHEAT oven to 450°F. Grease or lightly coat 13×9-inch baking dish with nonstick cooking spray; set aside.

COOK and stir beef and onions in large skillet over medium-high heat until no longer pink. Drain and discard fat. Stir in garlic salt and pepper.

BRUSH one side of each tortilla with oil. Spoon ¼ cup beef mixture off-center on oiled side of each tortilla. Top each with 1 tablespoon salsa, 1 tablespoon Cheddar cheese and 1 tablespoon Monterey Jack cheese. Fold ends of tortilla to middle, then roll tightly around mixture. Secure with toothpick. Place in prepared baking dish. Repeat with remaining tortillas. Brush tops with remaining oil.

BAKE, uncovered, 10 to 15 minutes or until lightly browned. Sprinkle with remaining cheeses. Bake 2 to 3 minutes longer or until cheese is melted. Remove toothpicks. Serve warm on bed of lettuce and tomatoes. Spoon remaining salsa over chimichangas. Serve with guacamole.

shrimp fettuccine

Makes 6 servings

8 ounces dry fettuccine
1 tablespoon olive oil
2 cloves garlic, finely chopped
2 tablespoons all-purpose flour
⅛ teaspoon ground black pepper
1 cup NESTLÉ® CARNATION® Evaporated Lowfat 2% Milk
¾ cup vegetable or chicken broth
½ cup (1.5 ounces) plus 2 tablespoons shredded Parmesan cheese, *divided*
½ pound cooked medium shrimp
½ cup chopped red bell pepper
   Fresh whole or finely sliced basil leaves for garnish (optional)

PREPARE pasta according to package directions; drain.

MEANWHILE, HEAT oil and garlic in medium saucepan over medium heat until garlic is fragrant. Stir in flour and black pepper; cook, stirring constantly, for 30 seconds. Add evaporated milk and broth. Cook, stirring constantly, for about 8 minutes or until mixture comes to a gentle boil and thickens slightly. Stir in ½ *cup* cheese until melted. Add shrimp and bell pepper; heat for an additional minute or until shrimp are warm.

TOSS with pasta. Top with *remaining 2 tablespoons* cheese and basil. Serve immediately.

Tip: Though more expensive, freshly grated Parmesan cheese has better flavor and texture than the canned kind. The most authentic variety is Parmigiano-Reggiano, which refers to the area in Italy where it comes from.

cheesy chimichangas

mexican tortilla stack

Makes 6 servings

1½ pounds lean ground beef
½ pound (8 ounces) VELVEETA®
    2% Milk Pasteurized Prepared
    Cheese Product, cut into ½-inch
    cubes
3 cups frozen corn
1 jar (16 ounces) TACO BELL® HOME
    ORIGINALS® Thick 'N Chunky
    Medium Salsa
12 corn tortillas, cut into quarters
⅓ cup BREAKSTONE'S® or
    KNUDSEN® Sour Cream

HEAT oven to 400°F. Brown meat in
large skillet; drain. Add VELVEETA®;
cook and stir until melted. Stir in corn
and salsa.

SPREAD one fourth of meat mixture
onto bottom of 13×9-inch baking
dish; top with 16 tortilla pieces. Repeat
layers 2 times. Top with remaining meat
mixture; cover tightly with foil.

BAKE 30 minutes. Top each serving
with sour cream.

Special Extra: Prepare as directed,
spreading one third of a 16-ounce can
of TACO BELL® HOME ORIGINALS®
Refried Beans onto each tortilla layer
before topping with the meat mixture.

louisiana gumbo

louisiana gumbo

Makes 6 servings

2 cups MINUTE® White Rice,
    uncooked
2 tablespoons butter
2 tablespoons all-purpose flour
½ cup onion, chopped
½ cup celery, chopped
½ cup green bell pepper, chopped
1 clove garlic, minced
1 package (14 ounces) smoked
    turkey sausage, sliced
1 can (14½ ounces) diced tomatoes
1 can (14½ ounces) chicken broth
1 package (10 ounces) frozen sliced
    okra, thawed*
1 tablespoon Cajun seasoning
¼ teaspoon dried thyme
½ pound raw shrimp, peeled,
    deveined
    Salt and black pepper, to taste

*Or substitute 1 package (10 ounces) frozen cut
green beans.

Prepare rice according to package
directions.

Melt butter in large skillet over
medium-high heat. Stir in flour; cook
and stir until light golden brown, about
5 minutes. Add onions, celery, bell
peppers and garlic; cook 2 to 3 minutes
or until tender.

Stir in sausage, tomatoes, broth, okra,
seasoning and thyme; cover. Simmer
5 minutes, stirring occasionally.

Add shrimp; cook 5 minutes or until
shrimp are pink. Season with salt and
pepper to taste. Serve with rice.

pepper steak

Makes 4 to 6 servings

1 pound boneless beef sirloin steak, thinly sliced
2 teaspoons ground paprika
2 tablespoons butter or margarine
1 (12-ounce) jar HEINZ® HomeStyle Savory Beef Gravy
2 tablespoons soy sauce
½ green bell pepper, cut into strips
½ red bell pepper, cut into strips
½ cup sliced green onions

Sprinkle steak with paprika; let stand 5 minutes. In large skillet, cook steak in melted butter until browned. Stir in gravy and soy sauce. Cover and simmer 15 minutes or until steak is tender. Add bell pepper strips and green onions. Cover and cook until bell pepper strips are crisp-tender.

easy chorizo-black bean burritos

Makes 6 servings

1 package (about 15 ounces) chorizo sausage, casings removed
1 can (about 15 ounces) black beans, rinsed and drained
Salt and black pepper
6 large flour tortillas
Crumbled queso fresco, sour cream and sliced avocado

1. Brown chorizo in large nonstick skillet over medium heat 6 to 8 minutes, stirring to break up meat. Drain fat. Add beans; cook until heated through. Mash mixture with a fork. Season with salt and pepper.

2. Spread chorizo mixture evenly on tortillas, leaving 1-inch border. Roll up tortillas; serve immediately. Serve with queso fresco, sour cream and avocado.

meatball bake

meatball bake

Makes 6 servings

1 jar (1 pound 10 ounces) RAGÚ® Chunky Pasta Sauce
2 cups water
2 cups uncooked instant rice
1 cup frozen green peas, thawed
1½ cups shredded mozzarella cheese (about 6 ounces)
1 package (12 ounces) frozen fully cooked cocktail-size meatballs, thawed

1. Preheat oven to 375°F. Spray 13×9-inch glass baking dish with nonstick cooking spray; set aside.

2. In large bowl, combine Pasta Sauce, water, rice, peas, 1 cup cheese and meatballs. Spoon into prepared baking dish.

3. Bake, uncovered, 25 minutes. Sprinkle with remaining ½ cup cheese and bake an additional 5 minutes or until cheese is melted. Let stand 5 minutes before serving.

Prep Time: 10 minutes
Cook Time: 30 minutes

chicken with grilled pineapple salsa

Makes 4 servings

1¼ cups WISH-BONE® Italian or Robusto Italian Dressing
¼ cup firmly packed dark brown sugar
¼ cup plus 2 tablespoons chopped fresh cilantro
2 pounds chicken thighs
2 tablespoons orange juice
¼ teaspoon salt
⅛ teaspoon ground red pepper
1 medium pineapple, peeled and cut into ¾-inch-thick slices
1 large red onion, cut into ½-inch-thick slices

1. Blend WISH-BONE® Italian Dressing, sugar and ¼ cup cilantro for marinade. Pour ¾ cup marinade over chicken in large, shallow nonaluminum baking dish or plastic bag; turn to coat. Cover, or close bag, and marinate in refrigerator, turning occasionally, 3 to 24 hours. Refrigerate remaining marinade.

2. Combine 2 tablespoons refrigerated marinade, remaining 2 tablespoons cilantro, orange juice, salt and pepper in medium bowl for salsa; set aside.

3. Remove chicken from marinade, discarding marinade. Grill or broil chicken, pineapple and onion, turning once and brushing frequently with remaining refrigerated marinade. Grill until pineapple and onion are tender and chicken is thoroughly cooked. Chop pineapple and onion and toss with salsa mixture. Serve salsa with chicken.

best-ever roast

Makes 6 to 8 servings

1 beef chuck shoulder roast (3 to 5 pounds)
1 can (10¾ ounces) condensed cream of mushroom soup, undiluted
1 package (1 ounce) dry onion soup mix
4 to 5 medium potatoes, quartered
4 cups baby carrots

Slow Cooker Directions
1. Place roast in **CROCK-POT®** slow cooker. (If necessary, cut roast in half to fit into **CROCK-POT®** slow cooker.) Combine mushroom soup and onion soup mix in medium bowl. Pour over roast. Cover; cook on LOW 4 hours.

2. Add potatoes and carrots. Cover; cook 2 hours.

cheesy cheeseburger mac

Makes 4 servings

1 pound ground beef
1¼ cups water
¾ cup milk
⅓ cup ketchup
1 package (12 ounces) VELVEETA® Shells & Cheese Dinner
1 large tomato, chopped

BROWN meat in large skillet; drain.

ADD water, milk and ketchup; mix well. Bring to boil. Stir in Shell Macaroni; return to boil. Reduce heat to medium-low; cover. Simmer 10 minutes or until macaroni is tender.

STIR in Cheese Sauce and tomatoes until well blended. Cook until heated through, stirring occasionally.

chicken with grilled pineapple salsa

forty-clove chicken

Makes 4 to 6 servings

1 cut-up whole chicken
(about 3 pounds)
Salt and black pepper
1 to 2 tablespoons olive oil
¼ cup dry white wine
2 tablespoons chopped fresh parsley
or 2 teaspoons dried parsley
flakes
2 tablespoons dry vermouth
2 teaspoons dried basil
1 teaspoon dried oregano
Pinch red pepper flakes
40 cloves garlic (about 2 heads),
peeled
4 stalks celery, sliced
Juice and peel of 1 lemon

Slow Cooker Directions

1. Remove skin from chicken. Sprinkle chicken with salt and pepper. Heat oil in large skillet over medium heat. Add chicken; brown on all sides. Remove to platter.

2. Combine wine, parsley, vermouth, basil, oregano and red pepper flakes in large bowl. Add garlic and celery; coat well. Transfer garlic and celery to **CROCK-POT®** slow cooker with slotted spoon. Add chicken to remaining herb mixture; coat well. Place chicken on top of celery mixture in **CROCK-POT®** slow cooker. Sprinkle lemon juice and peel over chicken. Cover; cook on LOW 6 hours.

forty-clove chicken

creole shrimp over creamy cheesy grits

Makes 6 servings

2 tablespoons olive oil
1 onion, diced
1 green bell pepper, diced
2 stalks celery, diced
2 tablespoons POLANER® Chopped
Garlic
1 (14-ounce) can diced tomatoes,
undrained
5 ounces frozen okra
2 teaspoons Creole seasoning
1 pound uncooked shrimp, cleaned,
peeled, deveined
1 cup water, divided
2 cups milk
½ cup CREAM OF WHEAT® Hot
Cereal (Instant, 1-minute,
2½-minute or 10-minute
cook time), uncooked
½ cup grated Parmesan cheese
½ teaspoon salt
Scallions, sliced (optional)

1. Heat olive oil in large skillet over medium heat. Add onion, bell pepper, celery and garlic. Cook and stir until vegetables are tender, about 4 minutes. Stir in diced tomatoes with juice, okra and Creole seasoning. Add shrimp and ½ cup water; stir and cover. Simmer 10 minutes. Remove cover and simmer 5 minutes longer.

2. Meanwhile, bring milk and remaining ½ cup water to a boil in saucepan. Stir in Cream of Wheat. Add cheese and salt; cook and stir until thickened.

3. Place serving-spoon-sized portion of grits on plate. Ladle shrimp over grits and top with sliced scallions, if desired.

Prep Time: 10 minutes
Start-to-Finish Time: 30 minutes

tandoori chicken kabobs

Makes 4 servings

2 ounces (¼ of 8-ounce package)
  PHILADELPHIA® Cream Cheese,
  softened
2 tablespoons tandoori paste
1 pound boneless skinless chicken
  breasts, cut into 2-inch pieces

MIX cream cheese and tandoori paste
in medium bowl. Add chicken; toss
to coat. Refrigerate 30 minutes to
marinate.

HEAT broiler. Remove chicken from
marinade; reserve marinade. Thread
chicken onto 4 skewers; brush with
reserved marinade. Place on rack of
broiler pan.

BROIL, 6 inches from heat source, 8 to
10 minutes or until chicken is done,
turning after 5 minutes.

oven-baked catfish

Makes 4 servings

1 cup PEPPERIDGE FARM®
  Corn Bread Stuffing, crushed
½ teaspoon paprika
1 egg
4 fresh or thawed frozen catfish
  fillets (about 1 pound)
2 tablespoons butter, melted
  Creamy ranch salad dressing

1. Stir the stuffing and paprika on a
plate. Beat the egg in a shallow dish
with a fork or whisk. Dip the fish into
the egg. Coat the fish with the stuffing
mixture. Place the fish onto a baking
sheet. Drizzle the fish with the butter.

2. Bake at 400°F. for 20 minutes or until
the fish flakes easily when tested with
a fork. Serve with the salad dressing for
dipping.

porcupine meatballs

porcupine meatballs

Makes 4 servings

1 tablespoon butter or margarine
1 small onion, chopped
1 pound lean ground beef*
1 cup MINUTE® White Rice,
  uncooked
1 egg, lightly beaten
1 packet (1½ ounces) meatloaf
  seasoning
¼ cup water
1 jar (14 ounces or larger) spaghetti
  sauce

*Or substitute ground turkey.

Melt butter in small skillet over
medium-high heat. Add onions; cook
and stir until tender.

Place onions, beef, rice, egg and
seasoning in large bowl. Add water;
mix until well blended. Shape into
medium-sized meatballs.

Pour spaghetti sauce into skillet. Bring
to a boil. Add meatballs; return to a
boil. Reduce heat to low; cover. Simmer
15 minutes or until meatballs are
cooked through.

zesty chicken & red pepper pasta

Makes 4 servings

½ cup roasted red peppers, drained
1 can (4 ounces) mild green chiles, drained
3 cloves garlic, minced
2 boneless, skinless chicken breast halves, cut into 1-inch cubes
8 ounces fettuccine noodles, cooked and drained
½ cup sun-dried tomatoes, rehydrated and chopped
½ cup sliced green onions
2 cups (8 ounces) SARGENTO® Shredded Reduced Fat 4 Cheese Italian Cheese, divided

COMBINE red peppers and chiles in blender or food processor; process until smooth (add up to ¼ cup water or chicken broth while processing if mixture is too thick); set aside.

COAT large nonstick skillet with cooking spray. Add garlic; cook 30 seconds over medium-high heat, stirring constantly. Add chicken; cook 5 minutes, or until browned on all sides, stirring frequently.

STIR fettuccine, sauce, tomatoes and onions into chicken. Cook 5 minutes, or until heated through, stirring frequently. Remove from heat. Stir in 1½ cups cheese. Top individual servings evenly with remaining cheese.

Prep Time: 25 minutes
Cook Time: 15 minutes

mexican picadillo

Makes 4 to 5 servings

1 pound lean ground beef
¾ cup diced onion
1 can (28 ounces) plum tomatoes, drained
½ cup seedless raisins
½ cup B&G® Pimento-Stuffed Olives, sliced
2 tablespoons REGINA® White Wine Vinegar
1 teaspoon ground cinnamon
1 teaspoon ground cumin
¾ teaspoon ORTEGA® Chili Seasoning Mix
Salt and black pepper, to taste
10 ORTEGA® Taco Shells
1 cup (4 ounces) shredded Cheddar cheese

PREHEAT oven to 225°F. Brown beef in medium skillet over medium heat. Add onions; cook and stir 5 minutes or until softened. Drain excess fat and discard. Add tomatoes, breaking up with wooden spoon. Stir in raisins, olives, vinegar, cinnamon, cumin, seasoning mix, salt and pepper. Bring mixture to a boil. Reduce heat; simmer, uncovered, 10 minutes.

PLACE taco shells on baking sheet; bake 5 to 10 minutes or until warmed. Fill shells with beef mixture and sprinkle with cheese.

Tip: Picadillo is a popular dish in Latin American countries. It is a mixture of ground meat and tomatoes, and its additional ingredients vary according to country or region. Picadillo is often served with rice and black beans or as a filling for tacos.

southwestern mac and cheese

southwestern mac and cheese

Makes 6 servings

1 package (8 ounces) elbow macaroni, uncooked
1 can (about 14 ounces) diced tomatoes with green peppers and onions
1 can (10 ounces) diced tomatoes with green chilies
1½ cups salsa
3 cups (about 12 ounces) shredded Mexican cheese blend, divided

Slow Cooker Directions
1. Lightly coat inside of **CROCK-POT®** slow cooker with nonstick cooking spray. Stir together macaroni, tomatoes, salsa and 2 cups cheese in prepared **CROCK-POT®** slow cooker. Cover; cook on LOW 3 hours and 45 minutes or until macaroni is tender.

2. Sprinkle remaining 1 cup cheese over contents of **CROCK-POT®** slow cooker. Cover; cook 15 minutes or until cheese on top melts.

spicy stir-fried shrimp

Makes 4 servings

1½ pounds large shrimp, peeled and deveined
3 tablespoons FILIPPO BERIO® Olive Oil, divided
1½ tablespoons curry powder
1 large red bell pepper, cut into strips
5 green onions, sliced into 1-inch strips
3 garlic cloves, minced
⅓ cup orange juice
1 tablespoon cornstarch, mixed with 2 tablespoons low-sodium soy sauce
Salt and pepper, to taste

Marinate shrimp with 2 tablespoons of olive oil and curry powder in a resealable plastic bag approximately 15 minutes.

In a large sauté pan over medium-high heat, heat remaining 1 tablespoon olive oil until hot. Add sliced red pepper and green onions, stirring 1 to 2 minutes. Add garlic and cook another minute. Remove red pepper mixture from pan and set aside in a bowl.

Place the pan back over the heat. When hot, add shrimp mixture; stir until shrimp are done. Pour in orange juice. When it starts to boil, add cornstarch mixture and thicken, stirring constantly. Add red pepper mixture back in and stir. Season with salt and pepper.

Serving Suggestion: Serve over basmati rice and top with sliced almonds.

spicy oriental stir-fry

Makes 4 servings

1 can (20 ounces) DOLE® Pineapple Chunks, undrained
½ cup ketchup
1 teaspoon sugar
1 teaspoon chili powder
1 teaspoon Worcestershire sauce
¼ teaspoon hot pepper sauce
2 tablespoons vegetable oil, divided
1 cup chopped green or red bell pepper
1 cup snow peas
1 pound boneless, skinless chicken breasts, cubed
¼ cup sliced DOLE® Green Onions
Hot cooked rice

• Drain pineapple; reserve 2 tablespoons juice.

• Stir together ketchup, reserved juice, sugar, chili powder, Worcestershire sauce and hot pepper sauce in bowl; set aside.

• Heat 1 tablespoon oil over medium-high heat in large skillet or wok. Add bell pepper; cook 1 to 2 minutes, stirring constantly. Add snow peas; cook 2 minutes more or until vegetables are tender-crisp. Remove vegetables from skillet.

• Add remaining 1 tablespoon oil to skillet; add chicken. Cook 3 to 4 minutes or until chicken is no longer pink. Stir in reserved sauce, pineapple chunks, green onions and vegetables; heat until hot. Serve over rice.

Substitution: You may substitute ½ (16-ounce) package frozen Oriental vegetable medley for bell peppers and snow peas, if desired. Add frozen vegetables in step 3 and cook 3 to 4 minutes. Proceed with step 4.

tuscan chicken simmer

Makes 4 servings

4 small boneless skinless chicken breast halves (1 pound)
4 ounces (½ of 8-ounce package) PHILADELPHIA® Cream Cheese, cubed
¼ cup water
¼ cup pesto
2 cups grape or cherry tomatoes
1 cup KRAFT® Finely Shredded Italian Five Cheese Blend

HEAT large nonstick skillet sprayed with cooking spray on medium-high heat. Add chicken; cover skillet with lid. Cook 5 to 7 minutes on each side or until chicken is cooked through (165°F). Remove chicken from skillet; keep warm.

REDUCE heat to medium. Add cream cheese, water, pesto and tomatoes to skillet. Cook, uncovered, 2 minutes or until heated through, stirring occasionally.

RETURN chicken to skillet. Cook and stir 1 minutes or until chicken is coated and heated through. Sprinkle with shredded cheese.

Prep Time: 5 minutes
Total Time: 25 minutes

spicy oriental stir-fry

beef and asparagus stir-fry

Makes 4 servings

¾ cup water
3 tablespoons soy sauce
3 tablespoons hoisin sauce
1 tablespoon cornstarch
1 tablespoon peanut or vegetable oil
1 pound beef sirloin, cut into thin strips
1 teaspoon dark sesame oil
8 shiitake mushrooms, stems removed and thinly sliced
1 cup baby corn
8 ounces asparagus (8 to 10 medium spears), cut into 1-inch pieces
1 cup snow peas or sugar snap peas
½ cup red bell pepper strips
½ cup cherry tomato halves (optional)
Hot cooked rice (optional)

1. Whisk water, soy sauce, hoisin sauce and cornstarch in small bowl until smooth. Set aside.

2. Heat peanut oil in large skillet or wok over medium-high heat. Add beef; cook and stir 5 to 6 minutes or until still slightly pink. Transfer to plate.

3. Add sesame oil, mushrooms and baby corn to skillet; cook and stir 2 to 3 minutes or until mushrooms are tender and corn is heated through. Add asparagus, snow peas and bell pepper; cook and stir 1 minute or until crisp-tender.

4. Return beef and any accumulated juices to skillet. Stir reserved soy sauce mixture and add to skillet with tomatoes, if desired. Cook and stir 1 minute or until heated through and sauce is thickened. Serve with rice, if desired.

orange-glazed mahi mahi with brown rice

Makes 4 servings

2 cups Florida orange juice
2 tablespoons honey
1 tablespoon tamari sauce*
1 teaspoon minced garlic
6 whole cardamom pods, cracked
2 whole cinnamon sticks
4 (4-ounce) mahi mahi fillets
Cooked brown rice

Low-sodium soy sauce may be substituted.

1. Preheat oven to 350°F.

2. In medium saucepan, combine orange juice, honey, tamari, garlic, cardamom and cinnamon. Bring to a simmer and cook until sauce thickens, about 15 to 20 minutes. Remove cardamom pods and cinnamon sticks from saucepan; cool glaze.

3. Remove ½ cup of glaze; set aside.

4. Place fish on foil-lined baking sheet and heavily coat with remaining glaze.

5. Bake fish 10 minutes per inch of thickness, or until light and flaky.

6. Place cooked fish over brown rice and baste with reserved glaze.

Favorite recipe from **Florida Department of Citrus**

Tip: Cardamom, a member of the ginger family, is commonly used in Indian cooking. It is an aromatic spice with a warm and slightly sweet flavor. Cardamom can be found in the pod or ground. If possible, buy only what you need for this recipe, as the flavor will fade quickly in your cupboard.

mostaccioli with smoked sausage and broccoli

mostaccioli with smoked sausage and broccoli

Makes 8 servings

1 package **HILLSHIRE FARM®** Smoked Sausage
1 package (16 ounces) uncooked mostaccioli noodles
3 cups small fresh broccoli pieces
⅛ teaspoon red pepper flakes (optional)
½ cup grated Romano or Parmesan cheese
⅓ cup heavy whipping cream

1. Cut sausage into ½-inch slices; set aside. Cook pasta in a large pan of boiling water according to package directions; drain and keep warm.

2. Heat a large nonstick skillet on medium-high heat for 3 minutes. Add sausage and broccoli; cook, stirring frequently, 4 to 5 minutes or until broccoli is tender. Add red pepper flakes, if desired; cook and stir 1 minute.

3. Gently toss together cooked pasta, sausage mixture, cheese and whipping cream in a large serving bowl.

steak soft tacos

Makes 4 servings

1 tablespoon vegetable oil
1 pound lean ground beef
½ cup water
1 cup salsa
1 packet (1¼ ounces) taco
   seasoning mix
2 cups MINUTE® White Rice,
   uncooked
8 flour tortillas
1 cup Cheddar cheese, shredded

Heat vegetable oil in large nonstick skillet over medium-high heat. Add beef; cook and stir until lightly browned. Stir in water, salsa and seasoning mix. Bring to a boil.

Stir in rice; cover. Remove from heat. Let stand 5 minutes. Fluff with fork.

Spoon ground beef mixture evenly onto tortillas; sprinkle with cheese. Fold tortillas in half to enclose filling.

wild west picante burgers

Makes 4 servings

1 pound ground beef
½ cup PACE® Picante Sauce
4 PEPPERIDGE FARM® Classic
   Hamburger Buns, split

1. Mix the beef and picante sauce thoroughly in a medium bowl. Shape the beef mixture firmly into 4 (½-inch thick) burgers.

2. Lightly oil the grill rack and heat the grill to medium. Grill the burgers for 10 minutes or until desired doneness, turning them over once halfway through grilling and brushing often with additional picante sauce.

3. Serve the burgers on the buns with additional picante sauce.

creamy chicken vegetable & noodles

Makes 6 servings

4 cups egg noodles, uncooked
1½ pounds boneless skinless chicken
   breasts, cut into 1-inch pieces
¼ cup KRAFT® Light Zesty Italian
   Dressing
3½ cups fresh broccoli florets
1 large red pepper, cut into strips
1 yellow squash, sliced
6 ounces VELVEETA® 2% Milk
   Pasteurized Prepared Cheese
   Product, cut into ½-inch cubes
1 tablespoon fat-free milk

COOK pasta as directed on package.

COOK chicken in dressing in large nonstick skillet on medium-high heat 5 to 7 minutes or until chicken is done, stirring occasionally. Stir in vegetables; cover. Simmer on medium heat 5 minutes or until vegetables are crisp-tender.

MICROWAVE VELVEETA® and milk in small microwavable bowl on HIGH 2 to 3 minutes or until VELVEETA® is melted and mixture is well blended, stirring after 1½ minutes. Add to chicken mixture; mix lightly. Serve over pasta.

Prep Time: 15 minutes
Total Time: 30 minutes

creamy chicken vegetable & noodles

hoisin barbecue chicken thighs

Makes 6 to 8 servings

⅔ cup hoisin sauce
⅓ cup barbecue sauce
3 tablespoons quick-cooking tapioca
1 tablespoon sugar
1 tablespoon soy sauce
¼ teaspoon red pepper flakes
12 skinless bone-in chicken thighs
      (3½ to 4 pounds total)
1½ pounds ramen noodles or other
      pasta
      Sliced green onions (optional)

Slow Cooker Directions

1. Combine hoisin sauce, barbecue sauce, tapioca, sugar, soy sauce and red pepper flakes in slow cooker until blended. Add chicken, meat side down. Cover; cook on LOW 8 to 9 hours.

2. Meanwhile, cook ramen noodles according to package directions. Serve chicken thighs over noodles. Sprinkle with green onions, if desired.

cheesy tuna dinner

Makes 4 servings

1 can (10¾ ounces) condensed cream
      of mushroom soup
1½ cups milk
2 cans (6 ounces each) tuna, drained,
      flaked
1 cup frozen green peas, thawed
2 cups MINUTE® White Rice,
      uncooked
1 cup Cheddar cheese, shredded
      Canned French-fried onions or
      crushed potato chips (optional)

Mix soup and milk in medium saucepan. Bring to a boil over medium heat, stirring frequently. Add tuna and peas; mix well. Return to a boil.

Stir in rice and cheese; cover. Reduce heat to low; cook 5 minutes. Stir until cheese is melted. Garnish with onions or chips, if desired.

creamy restaurant-style tortellini

Makes 6 servings

2 packages (9 ounces each)
      refrigerated three-cheese
      tortellini, uncooked
4 ounces (½ of 8-ounce package)
      PHILADELPHIA® Cream Cheese,
      cubed
1 cup milk
6 tablespoons KRAFT® 100% Grated
      Parmesan Cheese, divided
¼ teaspoon black pepper
1 bag (6 ounces) baby spinach leaves
1 cup quartered cherry tomatoes
      (about ½ pint)

COOK tortellini as directed on package.

PLACE cream cheese in large skillet. Cook on low heat until cream cheese is melted, stirring occasionally. Whisk in milk gradually. Stir in 4 tablespoons (¼ cup) of the Parmesan cheese and the black pepper. Add spinach; stir to coat. Drain pasta. Add to spinach mixture in skillet; mix lightly.

SPRINKLE with tomatoes and remaining 2 tablespoons Parmesan cheese just before serving.

Prep Time: 5 minutes
Cook Time: 15 minutes

hoisin barbecue chicken thighs

slow cooker southwestern pork roast

slow cooker southwestern pork roast

Makes 8 servings

2½ pounds boneless pork roast
1 envelope LIPTON® RECIPE SECRETS® Onion Soup Mix
1 can (14½ ounces) diced tomatoes, undrained
2 cans (4 ounces each) chopped green chiles, undrained
3 tablespoons firmly packed brown sugar
2 teaspoons chili powder
1 teaspoon ground cumin

Slow Cooker Directions

1. In slow cooker, arrange pork. Combine soup mix with remaining ingredients; pour over pork.

2. Cook, covered, on LOW 8 to 10 hours or on HIGH 4 to 6 hours or until pork is tender. Serve, if desired, with hot cooked rice or noodles.

hearty lasagna rolls

Makes 6 servings

1½ pounds ground beef
1 cup chopped fresh mushrooms
1 medium onion, finely chopped
1 small carrot, finely chopped
1 clove garlic, finely chopped
¼ cup dry red wine or beef broth
⅛ teaspoon cayenne pepper (optional)
2 cups shredded mozzarella cheese
1 egg, lightly beaten
5 tablespoons grated Parmesan cheese, divided
1 jar (1 pound 10 ounces) RAGÚ® Robusto!® Pasta Sauce
12 ounces lasagna noodles, cooked and drained

1. Preheat oven to 350°F. In 12-inch skillet, brown ground beef over medium-high heat; drain. Stir in mushrooms, onion, carrot and garlic; cook over medium heat, stirring occasionally, until vegetables are tender. Stir in wine and cayenne pepper; cook over high heat 3 minutes. Remove from heat; let stand 10 minutes.

2. In medium bowl, thoroughly combine ground beef mixture, mozzarella cheese, egg and 2 tablespoons Parmesan cheese. In 13×9-inch baking dish, evenly pour 2 cups Pasta Sauce. Evenly spread ⅓ cup ground beef filling over each lasagna noodle. Carefully roll up noodles. Place seam-side-down in baking dish. Evenly spread remaining sauce over lasagna rolls. Bake covered 40 minutes. Sprinkle with remaining 3 tablespoons Parmesan cheese and bake uncovered 5 minutes or until bubbling.

cornmeal-crusted catfish

Makes 4 servings

½ cup cornmeal
¼ cup crushed pecans
2 teaspoons dried minced onion
1½ teaspoons garlic powder
1 teaspoon salt
1 teaspoon paprika
½ teaspoon black pepper
3 tablespoons mayonnaise
2 tablespoons apricot preserves or
    fruit spread
1 pound catfish fillets
    Nonstick cooking spray

1. Combine cornmeal, pecans, onion, garlic powder, salt, paprika and pepper in small bowl. Heat medium nonstick skillet over medium heat. Add cornmeal mixture. Cook and stir 3 minutes or until cornmeal begins to brown. Transfer to shallow bowl.

2. Combine mayonnaise and preserves in small cup. Brush on both sides of catfish fillets. Dredge fillets in toasted cornmeal mixture.

3. Spray same skillet with cooking spray; heat over medium heat. Add fillets; cook until browned on one side. Turn; cook until browned and fish begins to flake when tested with fork.

Tip: Catfish is almost always a farmed fresh-water fish. Mild-tasting and adaptable, catfish is most frequently breaded and fried. However, being firm in texture, it can also be baked, broiled, poached, smoked and even added to soups and stews.

pork tenderloin with creamy mustard sauce

Makes 4 servings

1 pound pork tenderloin
1 teaspoon vegetable oil
½ cup NESTLÉ® CARNATION®
    Evaporated Fat Free Milk
2 tablespoons Dijon mustard
2 to 3 green onions, sliced

CUT pork into 1-inch-thick slices. Place pork between two pieces of plastic wrap. Flatten to ¼-inch thickness using meat mallet or rolling pin. Season with salt and ground black pepper, if desired.

HEAT oil in large, nonstick skillet over medium-high heat. Add *half* of the pork; cook on each side for 2 minutes or until browned and cooked through. Remove from skillet; set aside and keep warm. Repeat with *remaining* pork.

REDUCE heat to low. Add evaporated milk; stir to loosen brown bits from bottom of skillet. Stir in mustard and green onions. Return pork to skillet. Cook for 1 to 2 minutes or until sauce is slightly thickened, turning pork to coat with sauce.

cornmeal-crusted catfish

peanutty thai pasta

Makes 4 servings

8 ounces uncooked spaghetti
½ cup half-and-half
¼ cup creamy peanut butter
1 tablespoon honey
2 teaspoons soy sauce
1 teaspoon lemon juice
1 teaspoon minced fresh ginger
⅛ teaspoon red pepper flakes
1 cup shredded carrots
¼ cup sliced green onions
  Chopped peanuts
  Chopped fresh cilantro

1. Cook spaghetti according to package directions. Drain; cover and keep warm.

2. Combine half-and-half, peanut butter, honey, soy sauce, lemon juice, ginger and red pepper flakes in medium saucepan. Cook and stir over medium heat 4 minutes or until smooth and creamy.

3. Pour sauce over spaghetti. Add carrots and green onions; mix well. Sprinkle with peanuts and cilantro.

salmon with lemon-dill sauce

Makes 6 servings

6 tablespoons HELLMANN'S® or
  BEST FOODS® Low Fat
  Mayonnaise Dressing
2 teaspoons lemon juice
¾ teaspoon chopped fresh dill or
  ¼ teaspoon dried dill weed
1 small tomato, seeded and diced
6 salmon or halibut steaks, ¾ inch
  thick (about 4 ounces each)

1. In small bowl, combine HELLMANN'S® or BEST FOODS® Low Fat Mayonnaise Dressing, lemon juice and dill; reserve 2 tablespoons. Stir tomato into remaining mayonnaise mixture; set aside.

2. Brush salmon with reserved 2 tablespoons mayonnaise mixture. Grill or broil salmon, turning once, 8 minutes or until salmon flakes with a fork. Serve salmon with mayonnaise-tomato sauce.

Prep Time: 10 minutes
Cook Time: 8 minutes

home-style beef brisket

Makes 8 servings

1 envelope LIPTON® RECIPE
  SECRETS® Onion Soup Mix*
¾ cup water
½ cup ketchup
1 teaspoon garlic powder
½ teaspoon black pepper
1 (3-pound) boneless brisket of beef

Also terrific with LIPTON® RECIPE SECRETS® Onion Mushroom, Beefy Onion or Savory Herb with Garlic Soup Mix.

1. Preheat oven to 325°F. In 13×9-inch baking or roasting pan, add soup mix blended with water, ketchup, garlic powder and pepper.

2. Add brisket; turn to coat.

3. Loosely cover with aluminum foil and bake 3 hours or until brisket is tender. If desired, thicken gravy.

Tip: For a quick one-dish dinner, add 1 pound potatoes, cut into 2-inch chunks, and ½ pound carrots, cut into 2-inch pieces, to the baking pan with brisket during last hour of baking.

spicy peanut-coconut shrimp

Makes 4 servings

¼ cup shredded coconut
2 teaspoons dark sesame oil
1 pound large raw shrimp, peeled, deveined and patted dry
¼ to ½ teaspoon red pepper flakes
2 tablespoons chopped fresh cilantro
¼ cup chopped lightly salted roasted peanuts
Lime wedges (optional)

1. Toast coconut in large nonstick skillet over medium-high heat 2 to 3 minutes or until golden, stirring constantly. Immediately remove from skillet.

2. Heat oil in same skillet over medium-high heat. Add shrimp and red pepper flakes; stir-fry 3 to 4 minutes or until shrimp are pink and opaque. Add cilantro; toss well. Top with toasted coconut and chopped peanuts. Garnish with lime wedges.

turkey scaloppine with lemon

Makes 4 to 6 servings

½ cup flour
1½ to 2 pounds turkey scaloppine
Salt
2 tablespoons FILIPPO BERIO® Extra Light Olive Oil or FILIPPO BERIO® Olive Oil
⅓ cup water
4 to 6 lemon wedges

Place flour on a large sheet of waxed paper. Lay an empty sheet of waxed paper beside it. Season scaloppine on both sides with salt. Dip into flour to coat both sides. Shake off excess and place scaloppine on the empty sheet.

Heat oil in a large sauté pan over medium-high heat until very hot. Add scaloppine in a single layer. Cook 1 to 2 minutes on each side, or until browned. Remove scaloppine to plates or a serving platter. Add water to the pan. Scrape bottom of pan to remove any browned bits. Bring to a boil. Pour over scaloppine. Serve each portion with a lemon wedge.

mediterranean grilled steak

Makes 6 servings

½ cup WISH-BONE® Italian or Robusto Italian Dressing
2 large cloves garlic, finely chopped
2 teaspoons finely chopped fresh rosemary leaves *or* ½ teaspoon dried rosemary leaves, crushed
1½ pounds top sirloin steak, 1-inch thick

1. For marinade, combine WISH-BONE® Italian Dressing, garlic and rosemary. In large, shallow nonaluminum baking dish or plastic bag, pour ¼ cup marinade over steak; turn to coat. Cover, or close bag, and marinate in refrigerator 30 minutes. Refrigerate remaining marinade.

2. Remove steak from marinade, discarding marinade. Grill steak, turning occasionally and brushing frequently with refrigerated marinade, until desired doneness.

spicy peanut-coconut shrimp

chicken prosciutto roll-ups

oven-fried rosemary chicken

Makes 8 servings

½ cup plain dry bread crumbs
¾ teaspoon seasoned salt
½ teaspoon dried rosemary leaves, crushed
¼ teaspoon pepper
3½ pounds chicken parts, skin removed
½ cup HELLMANN'S® or BEST FOODS® Mayonnaise Dressing with Extra Virgin Olive Oil

1. Preheat oven to 400°F.

2. In shallow dish, combine bread crumbs, seasoned salt, rosemary and pepper; set aside.

3. In large plastic bag, add chicken and HELLMANN'S® or BEST FOODS® Extra Virgin Olive Oil Mayonnaise; shake to evenly coat. Remove chicken, then lightly dip in crumb mixture. On cookie sheet, arrange chicken.

4. Bake 40 minutes or until chicken is thoroughly cooked.

Prep Time: 10 minutes
Cook Time: 40 minutes

chicken prosciutto roll-ups

Makes 4 servings

1 can (28 ounces) tomato sauce
2 cloves garlic, minced
1 teaspoon dried oregano
1 teaspoon dried basil
4 boneless skinless chicken breasts
8 slices prosciutto
1 jar (12 ounces) roasted red peppers, drained and halved
1 cup grated Asiago cheese, divided
Hot cooked spaghetti

1. Preheat oven to 350°F. Combine tomato sauce, garlic, oregano and basil in medium bowl. Spoon 1 cup sauce into 3-quart casserole; set aside. Reserve remaining sauce.

2. Slice each chicken breast in half horizontally to make 8 thin pieces. Cover chicken with plastic wrap. Using flat side of meat mallet or rolling pin, pound each piece to ¼-inch thickness.

3. Place prosciutto slice (fold in half to fit), 1 roasted pepper half and 1 tablespoon cheese on each piece of chicken. Roll up, starting from longer side. Place rolls, seam sides down, in prepared casserole. Pour reserved sauce over chicken.

4. Cover; bake 50 minutes or until chicken is no longer pink in center. Sprinkle with remaining ½ cup cheese. Bake, uncovered, 10 minutes or until cheese is melted. Slice chicken rolls; serve with sauce over spaghetti.

desserts

desserts

· · · · ·

european mocha fudge cake

Makes 10 to 12 servings

1¼ cups (2½ sticks) butter or margarine
¾ cup HERSHEY'S SPECIAL DARK® Cocoa
4 eggs
¼ teaspoon salt
1 teaspoon vanilla extract
2 cups sugar
1 cup all-purpose flour
1 cup finely chopped pecans
Creamy Coffee Filling (recipe follows)
Chocolate curls (optional)

1. Heat oven to 350°F. Butter bottoms and sides of two 9-inch round baking pans. Line bottoms with wax paper; butter paper.

2. Melt butter in small saucepan; remove from heat. Add cocoa, stirring until blended; cool slightly. Beat eggs in large bowl until foamy; add salt and vanilla. Gradually add sugar, beating well. Add cooled chocolate mixture; blend thoroughly. Fold in flour. Stir in pecans. Pour mixture into prepared pans.

3. Bake 20 to 25 minutes or until wooden pick inserted in center comes out clean. Do not overbake. Cool 5 minutes; remove from pans to wire racks. Carefully peel off paper. Cool completely. Spread Creamy Coffee Filling between layers, over top and sides of cake. Garnish with chocolate curls, if desired. Refrigerate 1 hour or longer before serving.

creamy coffee filling

1½ cups cold whipping cream
⅓ cup packed light brown sugar
2 teaspoons powdered instant coffee

Combine all ingredients; stir until instant coffee is almost dissolved. Beat until stiff.   *Makes about 3 cups*

Make-Ahead Directions: Cooled cake may be wrapped and frozen up to 4 weeks; thaw, wrapped, before filling and frosting.

pistachio-strawberry cream cupcakes

Makes 18 cupcakes

1½ cups cake flour
¾ teaspoon baking powder
¼ teaspoon salt
1¼ cups granulated sugar
1 cup (2 sticks) butter, softened
4 eggs
1 tablespoon plus ½ teaspoon
    vanilla, divided
¼ cup chopped pistachios
1 package (4-serving size)
    cook-and-serve vanilla pudding
    and pie filling mix
1 cup whipping cream
2 tablespoons powdered sugar
½ cup diced strawberries
9 strawberries, halved

1. Preheat oven to 325°F. Line 18 standard (2½-inch) muffin cups with paper baking cups. Whisk flour, baking powder and salt in medium bowl until blended.

pistachio-strawberry cream cupcakes

2. Beat granulated sugar and butter in large bowl with electric mixer at medium speed until light and fluffy. Add eggs, one at a time, beating well after each addition. Add flour mixture; beat at low speed until just combined. Add 1 tablespoon vanilla; beat 30 seconds. Fold in pistachios.

3. Pour batter evenly into prepared muffin cups. Bake 20 minutes or until toothpick inserted into centers comes out clean. Cool in pans 10 minutes. Remove to wire racks; cool completely.

4. Prepare pudding mix according to package directions. Pour into medium bowl; cover surface of pudding with plastic wrap. Refrigerate until chilled. (Filling may be prepared up to 1 day ahead.)

5. Beat whipping cream, powdered sugar and remaining ½ teaspoon vanilla in medium bowl at high speed until soft peaks form.

6. To serve, remove paper baking cups. Halve cupcakes horizontally. Fold diced strawberries into 1 cup pudding. (Reserve leftover pudding for another use.) Place dollop of pudding mixture onto each cupcake bottom; cover with tops. Top each with dollop of whipped cream mixture and strawberry half.

Bake Time: 20 minutes

Tip: Cake flour is made from low-gluten soft wheat. It has a fine, delicate texture and low protein content, which makes it well suited for making tender cakes, cookies and other baked goods.

mini oreo® surprise cupcakes

Makes 24 servings

- 1 package (2-layer size) chocolate cake mix
- 1 package (8 ounces) PHILADELPHIA® Cream Cheese, softened
- 1 egg
- 2 tablespoons sugar
- 48 Mini OREO® Bite Size Chocolate Sandwich Cookies
- 1½ cups thawed COOL WHIP® Whipped Topping

PREHEAT oven to 350°F. Prepare cake batter as directed on package; set aside. Beat cream cheese, egg and sugar until well blended.

SPOON cake batter into 24 paper- or foil-lined 2½-inch muffin cups, filling each cup about half full. Top each with about 1½ teaspoons of the cream cheese mixture and 1 cookie. Cover evenly with remaining cake batter.

BAKE 19 to 22 minutes or until wooden toothpick inserted in centers comes out clean. Cool 5 minutes; remove from pans to wire racks. Cool completely. (There may be an indentation in top of each cupcake after baking.) Top cupcakes with whipped topping and remaining cookies just before serving. Store in tightly covered container in refrigerator up to 3 days.

Prep Time: 10 minutes
Bake Time: 19 to 22 minutes

Tip: To make portioning the cream cheese mixture into cake batter easier, spoon it into large resealable plastic bag. Seal bag securely. Snip small corner of bag with scissors. Squeeze about 1½ teaspoons of the cream cheese mixture over batter in each muffin cup.

spiced gingerbread

Makes 20 servings

- 1½ cups bran flakes
- 1 cup milk
- 1½ cups all-purpose flour
- 2 teaspoons baking soda
- 1 teaspoon ground cinnamon
- 1 teaspoon ground ginger
- ½ teaspoon ground cloves
- 1 cup GRANDMA'S® Molasses
- ½ cup butter, melted
- 3 eggs
- Confectioners' sugar (optional)

Heat oven to 350°F. In large bowl, mix bran flakes and milk; let stand 5 minutes. In separate bowl, mix flour, baking soda, cinnamon, ginger and cloves; set aside. In another bowl, with electric mixer at medium speed, beat molasses, butter and eggs until smooth. Blend in bran and flour mixtures. Pour batter into greased and floured 13×9-inch baking pan.

Bake 40 to 45 minutes or until toothpick inserted in center comes out clean. Cool in pan 10 minutes. Remove from pan; cool completely on wire rack. Sprinkle with confectioners' sugar, if desired; cut into 2½×2-inch pieces to serve.

mini oreo® surprise cupcakes

dutch apple dessert

Makes 6 to 8 servings

5 medium apples, peeled, cored and
   sliced
1 (14-ounce) can EAGLE BRAND®
   Sweetened Condensed Milk
   (NOT evaporated milk)
1 teaspoon ground cinnamon
½ cup (1 stick) plus 2 tablespoons
   cold butter or margarine,
   divided
1½ cups biscuit baking mix, divided
½ cup firmly packed brown sugar
½ cup chopped nuts
   Vanilla ice cream (optional)

1. Preheat oven to 325°F. In medium
bowl, combine apples, EAGLE BRAND®
and cinnamon.

2. In large bowl, cut ½ cup (1 stick)
butter into 1 cup biscuit mix until
crumbly. Stir in apple mixture. Pour
into greased 9-inch square baking pan.

3. In small bowl, combine remaining
½ cup biscuit mix and brown sugar. Cut
in remaining 2 tablespoons butter until
crumbly; add nuts. Sprinkle evenly over
apple mixture.

4. Bake 1 hour or until golden. Serve
warm with ice cream (optional). Store
leftovers covered in refrigerator.

Microwave Method: In 2-quart round
baking dish, prepare as directed above.
Microwave on HIGH (100% power)
14 to 15 minutes, rotating dish after
7 minutes. Let stand 5 minutes.

Prep Time: 25 minutes

chocolate almond pound cake

Makes 12 to 16 servings

1¼ cups chopped natural almonds,
   divided
1 package DUNCAN HINES®
   Moist Deluxe® Devil's Food
   Cake Mix
1 package (4-serving size) chocolate
   instant pudding and pie filling
   mix
4 eggs
1 cup dairy sour cream
½ cup vegetable oil
2 teaspoons vanilla extract
1 cup semisweet mini chocolate
   chips
½ cup DUNCAN HINES® Vanilla or
   Milk Chocolate Frosting

1. Preheat oven to 350°F. Grease and
flour 10-inch bundt pan.

2. Spread almonds on baking sheet.
Toast in 350°F oven for 8 to 10 minutes
or until fragrant. Cool completely.
Arrange ¼ cup almonds evenly in pan.

3. Combine cake mix, pudding mix,
eggs, sour cream, oil and vanilla extract
in large bowl. Beat at medium speed
with electric mixer for 4 minutes. Stir
in chocolate chips and remaining 1 cup
toasted almonds. Pour into pan. Bake
at 350°F for 45 to 50 minutes or until
toothpick inserted in center comes out
clean. Cool in pan 25 minutes. Invert
onto serving plate. Cool completely.

4. Place Vanilla frosting in microwave-
safe bowl. Microwave at HIGH (100%
power) for 15 to 20 seconds. Stir until
smooth. Drizzle over cake.

fluffy peanut butter pie

fluffy peanut butter pie

Makes one (9-inch) pie

¼ cup (½ stick) butter or margarine

2 cups finely crushed crème-filled chocolate sandwich cookies (about 20 cookies)

1 (8-ounce) package cream cheese, softened

1 (14-ounce) can EAGLE BRAND® Sweetened Condensed Milk (NOT evaporated milk)

1 cup smooth or crunchy peanut butter

3 tablespoons lemon juice

1 teaspoon vanilla extract

1 cup (½ pint) whipping cream, whipped

1. In small saucepan over low heat, melt butter; stir in cookie crumbs. Press crumb mixture firmly on bottom and up side to rim of 9-inch pie plate; chill while preparing filling.

2. In large bowl, beat cream cheese until fluffy. Gradually beat in EAGLE BRAND® and peanut butter until smooth. Add lemon juice and vanilla; mix well. Fold in whipped cream. Pour into crust.

3. Chill 4 hours or until set. Garnish as desired. Store leftovers covered in refrigerator.

Prep Time: 20 minutes
Chill Time: 4 hours

plum pudding cakes

Makes 4 servings

¾ cup sugar, divided
¼ cup all-purpose flour
¼ teaspoon salt
¼ teaspoon ground cinnamon
3 tablespoons unsalted butter, melted
  Grated peel of 1 lemon
1 tablespoon lemon juice
1½ cups milk
3 eggs, separated
1½ cups finely chopped unpeeled plums (about 4)
  Ice cream, any flavor (optional)

1. Preheat oven to 350°F. Lightly coat four 6-ounce ramekins or custard cups with nonstick cooking spray.

2. Combine ½ cup plus 1 tablespoon sugar, flour, salt and cinnamon in large bowl. Add butter, lemon peel and lemon juice; mix well. Whisk milk and egg yolks in small bowl. Stir into flour mixture; set aside.

3. Beat egg whites in medium bowl with electric mixer at medium-high speed until soft peaks form. Beat in remaining 3 tablespoons sugar; continue beating until stiff peaks form. Gently fold into flour mixture until well blended.

4. Pour batter into prepared ramekins. Sprinkle with chopped plums. Place ramekins in 13×9-inch baking dish and place in oven. Add 1 inch hot water to baking dish. Bake 25 to 30 minutes or until cakes puff up and are firm. Let stand 10 minutes. Serve with ice cream, if desired.

butterscotch nut cookie tart

Makes 12 to 16 servings

1 refrigerated pie crust (½ of 15-ounce package)
½ cup (1 stick) butter or margarine, softened
2 eggs, beaten
2 teaspoons rum extract
1 cup sugar
½ cup all-purpose flour
½ teaspoon salt
1 cup chopped walnuts
¾ cup plus 2 tablespoons (½ of 11-ounce package) HERSHEY'S Butterscotch Chips
  Vanilla ice cream (optional)

1. Heat oven to 350°F. Unroll pastry; place in bottom and up sides of 9-inch springform pan.

2. Beat butter in medium bowl; add eggs and rum extract, blending well. Stir together sugar, flour and salt; beat into butter mixture. Stir in walnuts and butterscotch chips; spread in bottom of crust. Fold edges of crust loosely over filling, if desired.

3. Bake 45 to 50 minutes or until golden brown. Cool 10 minutes on wire rack; remove side of springform pan. Cool an additional hour. Best if served slightly warm. Cut into wedges and serve with vanilla ice cream, if desired.

butterscotch nut cookie tart

raspberry tiramisu trifle

Makes 6 servings

- 1 package (8 ounces) cream cheese, softened
- 1 cup confectioners' sugar
- ¼ teaspoon ground cinnamon
- 1 cup heavy cream, whipped
- 1 package (6 ounces) PEPPERIDGE FARM® Milano® Cookies
- ⅓ cup brewed black coffee
- 1 cup sweetened frozen raspberries, thawed and drained
- ¼ cup grated semi-sweet chocolate

1. Beat the cream cheese in a medium bowl with an electric mixer on medium speed until smooth. Beat in the sugar and cinnamon. Fold in the whipped cream.

2. Spoon **1 cup** cheese mixture into a 4-cup trifle bowl. Dip **6** of the cookies, one at a time, into the coffee and place over the cheese layer, overlapping slightly. Spoon **2 tablespoons** raspberries over the cookies. Repeat the layers. Spread the remaining cheese mixture over the top. Garnish with the remaining cookies and raspberries. Refrigerate for 1 hour.

3. Garnish with the chocolate before serving.

Tip: Heavy cream will whip faster when the bowl and beaters are cold. Place the bowl and beaters in the freezer for about 15 minutes before using, then use the cream right from the refrigerator.

pumpkin bread pudding

Makes 8 servings

- 2 cups whole milk
- ½ cup plus 2 tablespoons butter, divided
- 1 cup solid-pack pumpkin
- 3 eggs
- 1 cup packed dark brown sugar, divided
- 1 tablespoon ground cinnamon
- 2 teaspoons vanilla
- ½ teaspoon ground nutmeg
- ¼ teaspoon salt
- 16 slices cinnamon raisin bread, torn into small pieces (8 cups total)
- ½ cup whipping cream
- 2 tablespoons bourbon (optional)

Slow Cooker Directions

1. Lightly coat **CROCK-POT®** slow cooker with nonstick cooking spray.

2. Combine milk and 2 tablespoons butter in medium microwavable bowl. Microwave on HIGH 2½ to 3 minutes or until very hot.

3. Whisk pumpkin, eggs, ½ cup brown sugar, cinnamon, vanilla, nutmeg and salt in large bowl until well blended. Whisk in milk mixture until blended. Add bread pieces; toss to coat.

4. Transfer to **CROCK-POT®** slow cooker. Cover; cook on HIGH 2 hours or until knife inserted in center comes out clean. Turn off heat. Uncover; let stand 15 minutes.

5. Meanwhile, combine remaining ½ cup butter, ½ cup brown sugar and cream in small saucepan. Bring to a boil over high heat, stirring frequently. Remove from heat. Stir in bourbon, if desired. Spoon bread pudding into individual bowls and top with sauce.

raspberry tiramisu trifle

new york-style strawberry swirl cheesecake

harvest honey spice cake

Makes 12 servings

1 cup honey
⅓ cup vegetable oil
⅓ cup strong brewed coffee
3 eggs
2½ cups all-purpose flour
1½ teaspoons baking soda
1½ teaspoons ground cinnamon
¾ teaspoon ground nutmeg
½ teaspoon salt
2 cups peeled chopped tart apples
½ cup toasted slivered almonds
½ cup dried cranberries
    Powdered sugar
    Toasted sliced almonds, for garnish

Using electric mixer beat together honey, oil and coffee. Beat in eggs.

Combine dry ingredients; gradually add to honey-egg mixture, mixing until well blended. Stir in apples, almonds and cranberries.

Pour into lightly greased and floured bundt or tube pan. Bake at 350°F for 35 to 40 minutes or until toothpick inserted in center comes out clean. Remove from oven; cool on wire rack. Dust with powdered sugar; garnish with sliced almonds, if desired.

Favorite recipe from **National Honey Board**

new york-style strawberry swirl cheesecake

Makes 16 servings

1 cup HONEY MAID® Graham
    Cracker Crumbs
3 tablespoons sugar
3 tablespoons butter, melted
5 packages (8 ounces each)
    PHILADELPHIA® Cream Cheese,
    softened
1 cup sugar
3 tablespoons flour
1 tablespoon vanilla
1 cup BREAKSTONE'S® or
    KNUDSEN® Sour Cream
4 eggs
⅓ cup SMUCKER'S® Seedless
    Strawberry Jam

PREHEAT oven to 325°F. Line 13×9-inch baking pan with foil, with ends of foil extending over sides of pan. Mix cracker crumbs, 3 tablespoons sugar and butter; press firmly onto bottom of prepared pan. Bake 10 minutes.

BEAT cream cheese, 1 cup sugar, flour and vanilla in large bowl with electric mixer on medium speed until well blended. Add sour cream; mix well. Add eggs, 1 at a time, mixing on low speed after each addition just until blended. Pour over crust. Gently drop small spoonfuls of jam over batter; cut through batter several times with knife for marble effect.

BAKE 40 minutes or until center is almost set. Cool completely. Refrigerate at least 4 hours or overnight. Lift cheesecake from pan using foil handles. Cut into 16 pieces to serve. Store leftover cheesecake in refrigerator.

Substitution: You may substitute 1 bag (16 ounces) frozen fruit, thawed, drained and puréed, for the ⅓ cup jam.

amazing red devil's food cake

Makes 12 servings

2½ cups all-purpose flour
½ cup unsweetened cocoa powder
1½ teaspoons baking soda
¼ teaspoon salt
½ cup (1 stick) butter, softened
1¾ cups sugar
2 eggs
1 teaspoon vanilla extract
1½ cups CAMPBELL'S® Tomato Juice
Creamy Butter Frosting
(recipe follows)

1. Heat the oven to 350°F. Grease and flour 2 (8-inch) round cake pans.

2. Stir the flour, cocoa, baking soda and salt in a medium bowl.

3. Beat the butter and sugar in a large bowl with an electric mixer on medium speed until the mixture is light and fluffy. Beat in the eggs, one at a time, beating well after each addition. Beat in the vanilla extract.

4. Reduce the speed to low. Add the flour mixture alternately with the tomato juice, beating well after each addition. Pour the batter into the cake pans.

5. Bake for 35 minutes or until a toothpick inserted in the center comes out clean. Cool the cakes in the pans on wire racks for 10 minutes. Remove the cakes from the pans and cool completely on the wire racks. Frost and fill with the Creamy Butter Frosting. Refrigerate until ready to serve.

Creamy Butter Frosting: Place ¾ **cup** (1½ sticks) butter, softened, **1 package** (16 ounces) confectioners' sugar, ¼ **cup** milk, ½ **teaspoon** vanilla extract and ¼ **teaspoon** salt in a medium bowl.

amazing red devil's food cake

Beat with an electric mixer on low speed until the mixture is smooth. Increase the speed to medium, adding more milk, if needed, until desired consistency. Makes 2½ cups.

chocolate cherry cake

Makes 12 to 16 servings

1 package DUNCAN HINES®
Moist Deluxe® Devil's Food
Cake Mix
½ cup chopped maraschino cherries, well drained
2 cups frozen non-dairy whipped topping, thawed
1 container DUNCAN HINES®
Chocolate Frosting

1. Preheat oven to 350°F. Grease and flour two 9-inch round cake pans.

2. Prepare, bake and cool cake as directed on package. Fold maraschino cherries into whipped topping.

3. To assemble, place one cake layer on serving plate. Spread with whipped topping mixture. Top with second layer. Frost sides and top with frosting. Refrigerate until ready to serve.

fresh corn ice cream

Makes 6 servings

1 medium ear corn
1 cup whole milk, plus more if
    necessary
2 cups half-and-half
¼ cup granulated sugar
¼ cup packed light brown sugar
2 egg yolks
¼ teaspoon vanilla
¾ cup chopped salted pecans

1. Scrape kernels from corn into a nonaluminum saucepan. Add corncob. Pour in 1 cup milk. Partially cover and cook over very low heat 30 minutes. (If milk evaporates completely, add an additional ¼ cup.) Discard corncob.

2. Stir half-and-half, granulated sugar and brown sugar into corn mixture. Cook, uncovered, over low heat, stirring frequently, until sugars dissolve and liquid begins to simmer.

3. Beat egg yolks in small bowl. Pour about ½ cup corn mixture into egg yolks, stirring constantly. Pour egg yolk mixture into saucepan. Cook over medium heat 10 minutes or until slightly thickened, stirring occasionally. Remove from heat. Stir in vanilla.

4. Pour corn mixture into plastic container, cover and refrigerate until completely cold. (This can be done a day in advance.)

5. Process corn mixture in ice cream machine according to manufacturer's directions. When ice cream begins to firm, mix in pecans and finish processing.

triple-layer mud pie

Makes 10 servings

3 squares BAKER'S® Semi-Sweet
    Chocolate, melted
¼ cup canned sweetened condensed
    milk
1 OREO® Pie Crust (6 ounces)
½ cup chopped PLANTERS® Pecans,
    toasted
2 packages (3.9 ounces each)
    JELL-O® Chocolate Instant
    Pudding
2 cups cold milk
1 tub (8 ounces) COOL WHIP®
    Whipped Topping, thawed,
    divided

MIX chocolate and condensed milk. Pour into crust; sprinkle with nuts.

BEAT pudding mixes and milk with whisk 2 minutes; spoon 1½ cups over nuts. Stir half the whipped topping into remaining pudding; spread over pudding layer in crust. Top with remaining whipped topping.

REFRIGERATE 3 hours.

Tip: Toasting nuts intensifies their flavor and crunch. Toast nuts in a dry skillet over medium heat until golden brown, stirring frequently. Cool to room temperature before combining them with other ingredients.

raisin apple bread pudding

raisin apple bread pudding

Makes 8 servings

4 cups white bread cubes
1 medium apple, chopped
1 cup raisins
2 large eggs
1 can (12 fluid ounces) NESTLÉ®
   CARNATION® Evaporated Milk
½ cup apple juice
½ cup granulated sugar
1½ teaspoons ground cinnamon
1 jar caramel ice cream topping
   (optional)

PREHEAT oven to 350°F. Grease 11×7-inch baking dish.

COMBINE bread, apple and raisins in large bowl. Beat eggs in medium bowl. Stir in evaporated milk, apple juice, sugar and cinnamon; mix well. Pour egg mixture over bread mixture, pressing bread into milk mixture; let stand for 10 minutes. Pour into prepared baking dish.

BAKE for 40 to 45 minutes or until set and apples are tender. Serve warm with caramel topping.

shortcut carrot cake

Makes 18 servings

- 1 package (2-layer size) spice cake mix
- 2 cups shredded carrots (about ½ pound)
- 1 can (8 ounces) crushed pineapple, drained
- 1 cup PLANTERS® Chopped Pecans, divided
- 2 packages (8 ounces each) PHILADELPHIA® Cream Cheese, softened
- 2 cups powdered sugar
- 1 tub (8 ounces) COOL WHIP® Whipped Topping, thawed

PREHEAT oven to 350°F. Prepare cake mix batter as directed on package, stirring in carrots, pineapple and ¾ cup of the pecans until well blended. Pour into 2 (9-inch) square baking pans. Bake 25 to 30 minutes or until toothpick inserted in centers comes out clean. Cool.

BEAT cream cheese and sugar with electric mixer or wire whisk until well blended. Stir in whipped topping until well blended.

PLACE 1 cake layer on serving plate. Spread with 1½ cups of the cream cheese mixture. Carefully place second cake layer on top of first cake layer. Frost top and sides of cake with remaining cream cheese mixture. Garnish with remaining ¼ cup pecans. Refrigerate until ready to serve.

Prep Time: 30 minutes
Bake Time: 30 minutes

shortcut carrot cake

creamy fruit dip

Makes 1½ cups

- 1 package (8 ounces) cream cheese, softened
- 1 container (8 ounces) vanilla yogurt
- ½ cup honey
- 1 teaspoon WATKINS® Vanilla
- ½ teaspoon WATKINS® Ground Cinnamon
- ½ teaspoon WATKINS® Nutmeg

Beat cream cheese in medium bowl until smooth. Add yogurt, honey, vanilla, cinnamon and nutmeg; mix until blended. Cover and refrigerate at least 1 hour to blend flavors. Serve with fresh fruit dippers.

Tip: Honey can be stored up to a year in a cool, dark place in a tightly sealed container or jar. Do not refrigerate honey or it will become grainy and too thick to use. If honey crystallizes, microwave the opened container on HIGH for 20 to 60 seconds.

deep dark mousse

Makes 4 to 6 servings

¼ cup sugar
1 teaspoon unflavored gelatin
½ cup milk
1 cup HERSHEY'S SPECIAL DARK®
   Chocolate Chips
2 teaspoons vanilla extract
1 cup (½ pint) cold whipping cream
   Sweetened whipped cream
   (optional)

1. Stir together sugar and gelatin in small saucepan; stir in milk. Let stand 2 minutes to soften gelatin. Cook over medium heat, stirring constantly, until mixture just begins to boil.

2. Remove from heat. Immediately add chocolate chips; stir until melted. Stir in vanilla; cool to room temperature.

3. Beat whipping cream with electric mixer on high speed in large bowl until stiff peaks form. Add half of chocolate mixture and gently fold until nearly combined; add remaining chocolate mixture and fold just until blended. Spoon into serving dish or individual dishes. Refrigerate. Garnish with sweetened whipped cream, if desired, just before serving.

Tip: Mousse, a French word meaning frothy or foamy, is a name given to a light and airy dish that may be either sweet or savory. Sweet mousse is made by folding something foamy, such as whipped cream or beaten egg whites, into a cooked gelatin or egg yolk mixture that is flavored with chocolate or puréed fruit. Serve mousse cold for the best flavor.

pineapple rice pudding

Makes 8 servings

1 can (20 ounces) crushed pineapple
   in juice, undrained
1 can (13½ ounces) coconut milk
1 can (12 ounces) evaporated milk
¾ cup uncooked arborio rice
2 eggs, lightly beaten
¼ cup granulated sugar
¼ cup packed light brown sugar
½ teaspoon ground cinnamon
¼ teaspoon ground nutmeg
¼ teaspoon salt
   Toasted coconut* (optional)
   Pineapple slices (optional)

*To toast coconut, spread evenly on ungreased baking sheet. Toast in preheated 350°F oven 5 to 7 minutes, stirring occasionally, until light golden brown.

Slow Cooker Directions
1. Place pineapple with juice, coconut milk, evaporated milk, rice, eggs, granulated sugar, brown sugar, cinnamon, nutmeg and salt in CROCK-POT® slow cooker; mix well. Cover; cook on HIGH 3 to 4 hours or until thickened and rice is tender.

2. Stir until blended. Serve warm or chilled. Garnish with coconut and pineapple.

Prep Time: 5 minutes
Cook Time: 3 to 4 hours

fresh summer fruit fool

fresh summer fruit fool

Makes 4 servings

1 cup sliced peeled peaches
   (about 2 small)
1 cup sliced peeled plums
   (about 2 large)
1 cup fresh raspberries
8 tablespoons powdered sugar,
   divided
1 tablespoon fresh lime juice
1 cup whipping cream
   Grated lime peel (optional)

1. Process peaches, plums, raspberries, 6 tablespoons powdered sugar and lime juice in blender until smooth. Add additional sugar to taste, if necessary. Cover; refrigerate at least 1 hour or up to 1 day.

2. Beat cream in large bowl with electric mixer at high speed until soft peaks form. Add remaining 2 tablespoons powdered sugar; beat until stiff. Fold in fruit mixture. Spoon into 4 serving bowls; garnish with lime peel.

banana-sour cream cake

Makes 16 servings

1 package (2-layer size) yellow
   cake mix
3 eggs
1 cup mashed ripe bananas (about 3)
1 cup BREAKSTONE'S® or
   KNUDSEN® Sour Cream
¼ cup oil
1 package (8 ounces)
   PHILADELPHIA® Cream Cheese,
   softened
½ cup (1 stick) butter, softened
1 package (16 ounces) powdered
   sugar
1 cup finely chopped PLANTERS®
   Walnuts

HEAT oven to 350°F. Beat first 5 ingredients with mixer on low speed just until moistened, stopping frequently to scrape bottom and side of bowl. Beat on medium speed 2 minutes. Pour into greased and floured 13×9-inch pan.

BAKE 35 minutes or until toothpick inserted in center comes out clean. Cool completely.

BEAT cream cheese and butter with mixer until well blended. Gradually add sugar, beating well after each addition.

REMOVE cake from pan. Carefully cut cake crosswise in half using serrated knife. Place 1 cake half, top-side down, on plate; spread with some of the cream cheese frosting. Top with remaining cake half, top-side up. Spread top and sides with remaining frosting. Press nuts into sides. Keep refrigerated.

Tip: To neatly frost the cake, freeze cake layers about 20 minutes before frosting. This helps to set the crumbs on the cut edges of the cake layers so they don't pull up into the frosting.

brownie chocolate chip cheesecake

Makes one (9-inch) cheesecake

- 1 (19.5- or 22-ounce) package fudge brownie mix
- 3 (8-ounce) packages cream cheese, softened
- 1 (14-ounce) can EAGLE BRAND® Sweetened Condensed Milk (NOT evaporated milk)
- 3 eggs
- 2 teaspoons vanilla extract
- ½ cup miniature semisweet chocolate chips

1. Preheat oven to 350°F. Grease bottom only of 9-inch springform pan. Prepare brownie mix as package directs for chewy brownies. Spread evenly in prepared pan. Bake 35 minutes or until set.

2. In large bowl, beat cream cheese until fluffy. Gradually beat in EAGLE BRAND® until smooth. Add eggs and vanilla; mix well. Stir in chocolate chips. Pour into baked crust.

3. Reduce oven temperature to 300°F. Bake 50 minutes or until set.

4. Cool. Chill thoroughly. Remove side of springform pan. Garnish as desired. Store leftovers covered in refrigerator.

Note: Chocolate chips may fall to brownie layer during baking.

Prep Time: 20 minutes
Bake Time: 1 hour 25 minutes

rustic fall fruit tart

Makes 8 servings

- 1½ cups all-purpose flour
- ½ cup (1 stick) butter, softened
- ½ cup (½ of 8-ounce container) PHILADELPHIA® Cream Cheese Spread
- 4 medium plums, thinly sliced
- 2 medium nectarines, thinly sliced
- ½ cup sugar
- 1 tablespoon cornstarch
- 1 teaspoon ground ginger
- ⅓ cup apricot jam

PLACE flour, butter and cream cheese in food processor container; cover. Process, using pulsing action, until mixture is well blended and almost forms a ball. Shape dough into ball; wrap tightly with plastic wrap. Refrigerate 1 hour or until chilled.

PREHEAT oven to 400°F. Place pastry on lightly floured surface; roll out to 12-inch circle. Place on lightly greased baking sheet; set aside. Toss fruit with sugar, cornstarch and ginger. Arrange decoratively over crust to within 2 inches of edge of crust. Fold edge of crust over fruit.

BAKE 30 minutes. Remove from oven; spread fruit with jam. Serve warm or at room temperature.

rustic fall fruit tart

carrot ginger cupcakes

Makes 24 cupcakes

1 pound carrots
3 cups all-purpose flour
⅓ cup pecan chips
2 teaspoons baking powder
1 teaspoon *each* baking soda and salt
½ teaspoon ground cinnamon
1½ cups granulated sugar
1¼ cups plus 2 tablespoons butter,
    divided
1 tablespoon honey
4 eggs
    Grated peel of 2 oranges
    Juice of 1 orange
1 tablespoon plus 1 teaspoon vanilla,
    divided
1½ teaspoons grated fresh ginger
1 package (8 ounces) cream cheese,
    softened
2 teaspoons orange extract
3½ cups powdered sugar
    Chopped pecans

1. Preheat oven to 350°F. Line
24 standard (2½-inch) muffin cups with
paper baking cups. Grate carrots in food
processor; drain well.

2. Whisk flour, pecan chips, baking
powder, baking soda, salt and cinnamon
in medium bowl until blended.

3. Beat granulated sugar, 1 cup plus
2 tablespoons butter and honey in large
bowl with electric mixer at medium
speed until light and fluffy. Add eggs,
one at a time, beating well after each
addition. Add carrots, orange peel and
juice, 1 tablespoon vanilla and ginger;
mix well. Add flour mixture; mix until
just combined.

4. Spoon batter evenly into prepared
muffin cups. Bake 20 minutes or until
toothpick inserted into centers comes
out clean. Cool in pans 10 minutes.
Remove to wire racks; cool completely.

5. Beat cream cheese, remaining ¼ cup
butter, orange extract and remaining
1 teaspoon vanilla in another medium
bowl at medium speed until light and
fluffy. Gradually add powdered sugar,
beating well after each addition.

6. Frost cupcakes; sprinkle with chopped
pecans. Refrigerate until ready to serve.

grasshopper pudding pie

Makes 8 servings

4 FAMOUS® Chocolate Wafers,
    divided
1½ cups cold fat-free milk
¼ teaspoon peppermint extract
1 package (1 ounce) JELL-O®
    Pistachio Flavor Fat Free Sugar
    Free Instant Pudding
2 cups thawed COOL WHIP® Sugar
    Free Whipped Topping
1 square BAKER'S® Semi-Sweet
    Chocolate, chopped

CRUSH 2 wafers; sprinkle onto bottom
of 9-inch pie plate sprayed with cooking
spray.

BEAT milk, extract and pudding mix
with whisk 2 minutes. Stir in whipped
topping and chopped chocolate; spread
into pie plate. Top with remaining
wafers, cut into quarters.

FREEZE 6 hours or until firm. Remove
pie from freezer 10 minutes before
serving; let stand at room temperature
to soften slightly before cutting to serve.

Prep Time: 15 minutes plus freezing

carrot ginger cupcakes

triple chocolate pudding cake with raspberry sauce

luscious "cream puffs"

Makes 9 servings

1 sheet frozen puff pastry
  (½ of 17.3-ounce package),
  thawed
1 package (3.4 ounces) JELL-O®
  Vanilla Flavor Instant Pudding
1 cup cold milk
½ cup thawed COOL WHIP® Whipped
  Topping
1 square BAKER'S® Semi-Sweet
  Chocolate, melted

HEAT oven to 400°F.

UNFOLD pastry on lightly floured surface; roll to 10-inch square. Cut into 9 circles with 3-inch cookie cutter. Place, 2 inches apart, on baking sheet. Bake 10 minutes. Remove to wire racks; cool completely.

BEAT pudding mix and milk with whisk 2 minutes. Stir in whipped topping. Refrigerate 15 minutes.

CUT pastry circles horizontally in half; fill with pudding mixture. Drizzle with chocolate.

triple chocolate pudding cake with raspberry sauce

Makes 12 servings

Vegetable cooking spray
1 package (about 18 ounces)
  chocolate cake mix
1 package (about 3.9 ounces)
  instant chocolate pudding and
  pie filling mix
2 cups sour cream
4 eggs
1 cup V8® 100% Vegetable Juice
¾ cup vegetable oil
1 cup semi-sweet chocolate pieces
  Raspberry dessert topping
  Whipped cream

Slow Cooker Directions

1. Spray the inside of a 4-quart slow cooker with the cooking spray.

2. Beat the cake mix, pudding mix, sour cream, eggs, vegetable juice and oil in a large bowl with an electric mixer on medium speed for 2 minutes. Stir in the chocolate pieces. Pour the batter into the cooker.

3. Cover and cook on LOW for 6 to 7 hours or until a knife inserted in the center comes out with moist crumbs. Serve with the raspberry topping and whipped cream.

Prep Time: 10 minutes
Cook Time: 6 to 7 hours

Tip: You can use any chocolate cake mix and any chocolate pudding mix flavor in this recipe, so be sure to stock up on your favorites.

hidden berry cupcakes

Makes 16 cupcakes

1¾ cups all-purpose flour
1¼ cups granulated sugar
  1 tablespoon baking powder
  ½ teaspoon salt
  ⅓ cup (5 tablespoons plus
    1 teaspoon) butter, softened
  3 eggs
  ⅔ cup milk
  1 tablespoon vanilla
  1 cup QUAKER® Oats (quick or
    old fashioned, uncooked)
  ½ cup seedless strawberry or
    raspberry fruit spread
    Confectioners' sugar

1. Heat oven to 350°F. Line 16 medium muffin cups with paper or foil liners.

2. Combine flour, sugar, baking powder and salt in large bowl. Add butter and beat with electric mixer on low speed until crumbly, about 1 minute. Combine eggs, milk and vanilla in medium bowl; add to flour mixture. Beat on low speed until incorporated, then on medium speed 2 minutes. Gently fold in oats. Divide batter evenly among muffin cups, filling each about three-fourths full.

3. Bake 18 minutes or until a wooden pick inserted in center comes out clean. Remove from pan; cool completely on wire rack.

4. Using small sharp knife, cut cone-shaped piece from center of each cupcake, leaving ¾-inch border around edge of cupcake. Carefully remove and reserve cake pieces. Fill each depression with generous teaspoon of fruit spread. Top with reserved cake pieces; sift confectioners' sugar over tops of cupcakes.

chocolate chili and orange fondue

Makes 6 servings

  2 (4-ounce) 60 to 70% bittersweet
    chocolate bars, coarsely
    chopped
  2 tablespoons butter, softened
1½ cups (12 ounces) whipping cream
  ½ cup frozen orange juice
    concentrate
  1 teaspoon vanilla
  ½ teaspoon ancho or chipotle chili
    powder

1. Place chopped chocolate and butter in medium bowl.

2. Bring cream to a simmer in small saucepan over medium heat; pour over chocolate. Add orange juice concentrate, vanilla and chili powder. Stir until chocolate is melted and mixture is smooth. Serve immediately in individual bowls or fondue pot.

Tip: Serve fondue with an assortment of dippers that may include orange segments, apple slices, pear slices, pineapple chunks, banana chunks, strawberries, cookies, marshmallows, pound cake or angel food cake cubes and pretzels.

hidden berry cupcakes

plum bread pudding

Makes 12 to 16 servings

1 loaf (1 pound) sliced egg bread,
    lightly toasted
2 tablespoons unsalted butter,
    divided
12 large unpeeled Italian plums,
    pitted and cut into wedges
    (about 4 cups total)
1½ cups plus 2 tablespoons sugar,
    divided
3 cups half-and-half
10 eggs
1¼ cups milk
2 teaspoons vanilla
¾ teaspoon salt
¾ teaspoon ground cinnamon
    Sweetened whipped cream or
    vanilla ice cream (optional)

Slow Cooker Directions
1. Lightly coat inside of 6-quart
CROCK-POT® slow cooker with
nonstick cooking spray. Cut toasted
bread into 1-inch pieces.

2. Melt 1 tablespoon butter in large skillet
over medium-high heat. Add half of
sliced plums. Sprinkle with 1 tablespoon
sugar. Cook 2 minutes or until plums
give off juices. Pour plums and juices into
medium bowl; repeat with remaining
1 tablespoon butter, plums and
1 tablespoon sugar. Cool slightly.

3. Beat together half-and-half, eggs,
milk, remaining 1½ cups sugar,
vanilla, salt and cinnamon in large
bowl. Stir in bread cubes, plums and
any accumulated juices. Spoon into
prepared **CROCK-POT®** slow cooker.
Cover; cook on HIGH 3 hours or until
pudding is firm when gently shaken
and thin knife inserted halfway between
center and edge comes out clean.
Remove insert from base and cool
15 minutes. Serve with whipped cream
or ice cream, if desired.

ultimate chocolate caramel pecan pie

Makes 10 servings

3 cups chopped PLANTERS® Pecans,
    divided
¼ cup granulated sugar
¼ cup (½ stick) butter or margarine,
    melted
1 package (14 ounces) KRAFT®
    Caramels
⅔ cup whipping cream, divided
1 package (8 squares) BAKER'S®
    Semi-Sweet Chocolate
¼ cup powdered sugar
½ teaspoon vanilla

HEAT oven to 350°F.

BLEND 2 cups nuts in blender until
finely ground, using pulsing action. Mix
with granulated sugar and butter; press
onto bottom and up side of 9-inch pie
plate. Bake 12 to 15 minutes or until
lightly browned. Cool completely. (If
crust puffs up during baking, gently
press down with back of spoon.)

MICROWAVE caramels and ⅓ cup
whipping cream in microwavable bowl
on HIGH 2½ to 3 minutes or until
caramels are completely melted and
mixture is well blended, stirring after
each minute. Pour into crust. Chop
remaining nuts; sprinkle over caramel
layer.

COOK chocolate, remaining whipping
cream, powdered sugar and vanilla
in saucepan on low heat just until
chocolate is completely melted, stirring
constantly. Pour over pie; gently spread
to evenly cover top. Refrigerate 2 hours.

plum bread pudding

chocolate crème brulée

chocolate crème brulée

2 cups whipping cream
3 squares semisweet or bittersweet
   baking chocolate, finely chopped
3 egg yolks
¼ cup granulated sugar
2 teaspoons vanilla
3 tablespoons packed brown sugar

1. Preheat oven to 325°F. Bring cream to a simmer in medium saucepan over medium heat. Remove from heat; stir in chocolate until melted and smooth. Set aside to cool slightly.

2. Beat egg yolks and granulated sugar in large bowl with electric mixer at medium-high speed 5 minutes or until thick and pale yellow. Beat in chocolate mixture and vanilla until blended.

3. Divide mixture among four 6-ounce custard cups. Place cups in baking pan; place pan in oven. Pour boiling water into baking pan to reach halfway up sides of custard cups. Cover pan loosely with foil.

4. Bake 30 minutes or until edges are just set. Remove cups from baking pan to wire rack to cool completely. Wrap with plastic wrap and refrigerate 4 hours or up to 3 days.

5. When ready to serve, preheat broiler. Spread about 2 teaspoons brown sugar evenly over each cup. Broil 3 to 4 minutes, watching carefully, until sugar bubbles and browns. Serve immediately.

raspberry mousse

1 package (10 ounces) frozen
   raspberries in syrup
1 package (4-serving size) raspberry-
   flavored gelatin
¼ cup water
2 cups whipping cream

1. Process raspberries with syrup in food processor or blender until smooth. Press through fine mesh sieve to remove seeds. Set aside.

2. Heat gelatin and water in small saucepan over medium heat 5 to 7 minutes or until mixture is very syrupy, stirring occasionally. Remove from heat. Cool slightly.

3. Beat cream in large bowl with electric mixer at high speed 3 to 5 minutes or until soft peaks form. Add raspberries and gelatin mixture; beat 3 to 5 minutes or until well blended.

4. Pour into individual serving dishes; refrigerate 2 hours or until set.

cookies
& bars

cookies & bars

• • • • •

toasted coconut pinwheels

Makes about 3 dozen cookies

- 1¼ cups sweetened flaked coconut
- 1 package (about 18 ounces) white cake mix
- 1 package (8 ounces) cream cheese, softened
- ¼ cup all-purpose flour
- 1 teaspoon coconut extract or vanilla
- ¾ cup apricot jam

1. Preheat oven to 350°F. Spread coconut on baking sheet; bake 4 minutes. Stir; bake 4 minutes or until lightly browned. Cool completely.

2. Beat cake mix, cream cheese, flour and coconut extract in large bowl with electric mixer at low speed until well blended. Place dough between two sheets parchment paper and roll into rectangle about 13×10 inches. Spread jam over dough, leaving ½-inch border. Sprinkle with toasted coconut.

3. Roll dough jelly-roll style starting from long side. (Do not roll paper up with dough.) Wrap in plastic wrap; freeze 2 hours or refrigerate 4 hours or overnight.

4. Preheat oven to 350°F. Spray cookie sheets with nonstick cooking spray.

5. Slice dough into ¼-inch-thick slices; place 1 inch apart on prepared cookie sheets. Bake 12 to 15 minutes or until edges are just beginning to brown. Cool on cookie sheets 3 minutes. Remove to wire racks; cool completely.

chocolate chunk cookies

Makes 2 dozen cookies

1⅔ cups all-purpose flour
⅓ cup CREAM OF WHEAT® Hot
    Cereal (Instant, 1-minute,
    2½-minute or 10-minute
    cook time), uncooked
½ teaspoon baking soda
¼ teaspoon salt
¾ cup (1½ sticks) butter, softened
½ cup packed brown sugar
⅓ cup granulated sugar
1 egg
1 teaspoon vanilla extract
1 (11.5-ounce) bag chocolate chunks
1 cup chopped pecans

1. Preheat oven to 375°F. Lightly grease cookie sheets. Blend flour, Cream of Wheat, baking soda and salt in medium bowl; set aside.

2. Beat butter and sugars in large bowl with electric mixer at medium speed until creamy. Add egg and vanilla. Beat until fluffy. Reduce speed to low. Add Cream of Wheat mixture; mix well. Stir in chocolate chunks and pecans.

3. Drop by tablespoonfuls onto prepared cookie sheets. Bake 9 to 11 minutes or until golden brown. Let stand on cookie sheets 1 minute before transferring to wire racks to cool completely.

Prep Time: 15 minutes
Start-to-Finish Time: 35 minutes

Tip: Chocolate and pecans are classic cookie additions, but they can be substituted with other chunks, chips or nuts according to your taste.

peanut butter toffee bars

Makes 2 dozen bars

1 cup SKIPPY® SUPER CHUNK®
    Peanut Butter
½ cup SHEDD'S SPREAD COUNTRY
    CROCK® Spread, softened
¾ cup firmly packed light brown
    sugar
½ cup granulated sugar
1 teaspoon vanilla extract
2 eggs
2 cups all-purpose flour
½ teaspoon salt
1 package (12 ounces) semi-sweet
    chocolate chips
1 cup toffee bar bits

1. Preheat oven to 350°F. Grease 13×9-inch baking pan; set aside.

2. In large bowl, with electric mixer, beat SKIPPY® SUPER CHUNK® Peanut Butter, Spread, brown sugar, granulated sugar and vanilla until thick and creamy, about 5 minutes. Beat in eggs, then flour blended with salt. Stir in 1 cup chocolate chips. Evenly spread into prepared pan.

3. Bake 25 minutes or until lightly browned. Remove from oven to wire rack and immediately sprinkle with remaining 1 cup chocolate chips. Let stand 5 minutes. Evenly spread melted chocolate, then sprinkle with toffee bar bits; cool completely. To serve, cut into bars.

Prep Time: 15 minutes
Cook Time: 25 minutes

chocolate chunk cookies

caribbean crunch shortbread

Makes about 2 dozen cookies

- 1 cup (2 sticks) unsalted butter, softened
- ½ cup powdered sugar
- 2 tablespoons packed light brown sugar
- ¼ teaspoon salt
- 2 cups all-purpose flour
- 1 cup diced dried tropical fruit mix, such as pineapple, mango and papaya

1. Beat butter, powdered sugar, brown sugar and salt in large bowl with electric mixer at medium speed until creamy. Add flour, ½ cup at a time, beating after each addition. Stir in dried fruit.

2. Shape dough into 14-inch log. Wrap in plastic wrap; refrigerate 1 hour.

3. Preheat oven to 300°F. Cut log into ½-inch slices; place on ungreased cookie sheets. Bake 20 to 25 minutes or until cookies are set and lightly browned. Cool on cookie sheets 5 minutes. Remove to wire racks; cool completely.

walnut macaroons

Makes about 3 dozen cookies

- 2⅔ cups flaked coconut
- 1¼ cups coarsely chopped California walnuts
- ⅓ cup flour
- ½ teaspoon ground cinnamon
- ¼ teaspoon salt
- 4 egg whites
- 1 teaspoon grated lemon peel
- 2 (1-ounce) squares semisweet chocolate

Combine coconut, walnuts, flour, cinnamon and salt in large bowl. Add egg whites and lemon peel; mix well.

Drop teaspoonfuls of walnut mixture onto lightly greased baking sheets. Bake in 325°F oven 20 minutes or until golden brown. Remove from baking sheets immediately.

Place chocolate in small microwavable bowl. Microwave on HIGH until melted, about 1 minute; stir. Dip macaroon bottoms in chocolate. Place on waxed paper. Let stand until chocolate is set.

Favorite recipe from **Walnut Marketing Board**

banana rum brownies

Makes 16 servings

- 1 box (about 21 ounces) brownie mix
- ¼ cup chocolate milk or regular milk
- 1 tablespoon rum extract
- 3 DOLE® Bananas, cubed
- ½ cup toasted chopped pecans

• Prepare brownie mix as directed on package in large bowl; set aside.

• Heat milk and extract in medium saucepan until hot. Add bananas; stir for 1 minute to heat through.

• Pour banana mixture and nuts into brownie mix and stir. Pour into lightly greased 9-inch square pan.

• Bake at 350°F 35 to 40 minutes or until toothpick inserted in center comes out clean. Sprinkle with powdered sugar, if desired. Cut into bars.

Prep Time: 15 minutes
Bake Time: 35 to 40 minutes

double-drizzled chocolate shortbread cookies

double-drizzled chocolate shortbread cookies

Makes about 6 dozen cookies

2 cups (4 sticks) butter or margarine, softened
1⅓ cups sugar
1 teaspoon vanilla extract
4 egg yolks
4 cups all-purpose flour
½ cup HERSHEY'S SPECIAL DARK® Cocoa
1 teaspoon salt
1 cup chopped pecans
1 cup HERSHEY'S SPECIAL DARK® Chocolate Chips or HERSHEY'S Semi-Sweet Chocolate Chips
2 tablespoons shortening (do not use butter, margarine, spread or oil), divided
1 cup REESE'S® Peanut Butter Chips or HERSHEY'S Premier White Chips

1. Beat butter, sugar and vanilla until well blended. Add egg yolks, one at a time, beating well after each addition. Gradually add flour, cocoa and salt, beating until blended. (Batter is very stiff.)

2. Divide dough in half. Shape each part into 12-inch-long log. Roll each in pecans, pressing firmly to have pecans adhere. Wrap each roll separately in plastic wrap. Refrigerate 6 to 8 hours.

3. Heat oven to 350°F. Using a sharp knife, cut rolls into ⅜-inch slices. Place on ungreased cookie sheet. Bake 10 to 12 minutes or until set. Cool slightly. Remove from cookie sheet to wire rack. Cool completely.

4. Place chocolate chips and 1 tablespoon shortening in small microwave-safe bowl. Microwave at MEDIUM (50%) 1 minute; stir. If necessary, microwave at MEDIUM an additional 15 seconds at a time, stirring after each heating, until chips are melted and smooth when stirred. Drizzle over tops of cookies. Melt peanut butter chips or white chips with remaining 1 tablespoon shortening; drizzle over chocolate. Let stand until drizzles are set.

Tip: A decadent delight, shortbread is a thick, rich cookie made with a high proportion of butter to flour and sugar. Real butter should be used for the best flavor and texture. Be sure to allow plenty of time for the butter to soften at room temperature before you start working with it. Using the microwave to save time will lead to inferior results.

white chocolate cranberry dippers

Makes about 1½ dozen cookies

- 1 package (about 18 ounces) spice cake mix
- 1 cup old-fashioned oats
- ⅓ cup vegetable oil
- 2 eggs
- 1 teaspoon vanilla
- 1 cup dried cranberries
- 1 cup chopped walnuts or pecans (optional)
- 2½ cups white chocolate chips, divided
- 3 tablespoons vegetable shortening

1. Preheat oven to 350°F. Spray cookie sheets lightly with nonstick cooking spray.

2. Combine cake mix, oats, oil, eggs and vanilla in large bowl until well blended. Stir in cranberries, walnuts, if desired, and 1 cup white chocolate chips.

3. Drop by tablespoonfuls 2 inches apart onto prepared cookie sheets. Bake 10 minutes or until edges are lightly browned. Cool on cookie sheets 5 minutes. Remove to wire racks; cool completely.

4. Place remaining 1½ cups white chocolate chips and shortening in small microwavable bowl; microwave on HIGH 15 seconds. Stir until mixture is melted and well blended. (Heat additional 10 seconds if needed.)

5. Spread sheet of waxed paper on work surface. Dip each cookie into chocolate mixture and allow excess to drip into bowl. Place cookies on waxed paper until chocolate sets.

Prep Time: 25 minutes
Bake Time: 10 minutes

creamy cappuccino brownies

Makes 2 dozen brownies

- 1 package (21 to 24 ounces) brownie mix, plus ingredients to prepare mix
- 1 tablespoon coffee crystals *or* 1 teaspoon espresso powder
- 2 tablespoons warm water
- 1 cup (8 ounces) Wisconsin Mascarpone cheese
- 3 tablespoons granulated sugar
- 1 egg
  Powdered sugar

Grease bottom of 13×9-inch baking pan. Prepare brownie mix according to package directions. Pour half of batter into prepared pan. In medium bowl, dissolve coffee crystals in warm water; add Mascarpone, granulated sugar and egg. Blend until smooth. Drop by spoonfuls over brownie batter; top with remaining brownie batter. With knife, swirl cheese mixture through brownies creating marbled effect. Bake at 375°F 30 to 35 minutes or until toothpick inserted in center comes out clean. Sprinkle with powdered sugar.

Favorite recipe from **Wisconsin Milk Marketing Board**

white chocolate cranberry dippers

pumpkin-oatmeal raisin cookies

pumpkin-oatmeal raisin cookies

Makes 4 dozen cookies

2 cups all-purpose flour
1⅓ cups quick or old-fashioned oats
2 teaspoons pumpkin pie spice
1 teaspoon baking soda
½ teaspoon salt
1 cup (2 sticks) butter or margarine, softened
1 cup packed brown sugar
1 cup granulated sugar
1 cup LIBBY'S® 100% Pure Pumpkin
1 large egg
1 teaspoon vanilla extract
¾ cup chopped walnuts
¾ cup raisins

PREHEAT oven to 350°F. Lightly grease baking sheets.

COMBINE flour, oats, pie spice, baking soda and salt in medium bowl. Beat butter, brown sugar and granulated sugar in large mixer bowl until light and fluffy. Add pumpkin, egg and vanilla extract; mix well. Add flour mixture; mix well. Stir in nuts and raisins. Drop by rounded tablespoons onto prepared baking sheets.

BAKE for 14 to 16 minutes or until cookies are lightly browned and set in centers. Cool on baking sheets for 2 minutes; remove to wire racks to cool completely.

layers of love chocolate brownies

Makes 16 brownies

¾ cup all-purpose flour
¾ cup NESTLÉ® TOLL HOUSE®
    Baking Cocoa
¼ teaspoon salt
½ cup (1 stick) butter, cut into pieces
½ cup granulated sugar
½ cup packed brown sugar
3 large eggs, *divided*
2 teaspoons vanilla extract
1 cup chopped pecans
¾ cup NESTLÉ® TOLL HOUSE®
    Premier White Morsels
½ cup caramel ice cream topping
¾ cup NESTLÉ® TOLL HOUSE®
    Semi-Sweet Chocolate Morsels

PREHEAT oven to 350°F. Grease 8-inch square baking pan.

COMBINE flour, cocoa and salt in small bowl. Beat butter, granulated sugar and brown sugar in large mixer bowl until creamy. Add *2 eggs,* one at a time, beating well after each addition. Add vanilla extract; mix well. Gradually beat in flour mixture. Reserve ¾ *cup* batter. Spread *remaining* batter into prepared baking pan. Sprinkle pecans and white morsels over batter. Drizzle caramel topping over top. Beat *remaining* egg and *reserved* batter in same large bowl until light in color. Stir in semi-sweet morsels. Spread evenly over caramel topping.

BAKE for 30 to 35 minutes or until center is set. Cool completely in pan on wire rack. Cut into squares.

date bars

Makes 16 bars

1 package (8 ounces) chopped dates
¾ cup NESTLÉ® CARNATION®
    Evaporated Milk
2 tablespoons granulated sugar
1 teaspoon vanilla extract
½ cup (1 stick) butter or margarine,
    softened
½ cup packed light brown sugar
1 cup all-purpose flour
¾ cup quick oats
½ teaspoon baking soda
½ teaspoon salt
½ teaspoon ground cinnamon

PREHEAT oven to 400°F. Grease 8-inch square baking pan.

COMBINE dates, evaporated milk, granulated sugar and vanilla extract in medium saucepan. Cook over medium-low heat, stirring occasionally, for 8 to 10 minutes or until thickened. Remove from heat.

BEAT butter and brown sugar in large mixer bowl until creamy. Beat in flour, oats, baking soda, salt and cinnamon. With floured fingers, press *half* of crust mixture onto bottom of prepared baking pan. Spread date filling over crust. Top with *remaining* crust.

BAKE for 20 to 25 minutes or until golden. Cut into bars. Serve warm.

layers of love chocolate brownies

strawberry swirl cheesecake bars

Makes 2 to 3 dozen bars

- 1 (10-ounce) package frozen strawberries, thawed (2½ cups)
- 1 tablespoon cornstarch
- 1¾ cups finely crushed cinnamon graham cracker crumbs
- ¼ cup (½ stick) butter or margarine, melted
- 2 (8-ounce) packages cream cheese, softened
- 1 (14-ounce) can EAGLE BRAND® Sweetened Condensed Milk (NOT evaporated milk)
- 2 eggs
- ⅓ cup lemon juice
- 1 teaspoon vanilla extract

1. Preheat oven to 350°F. In blender container, blend strawberries until smooth. In saucepan over medium heat, combine strawberry purée and cornstarch; cook and stir until thickened. Cool.

2. In small bowl, combine graham cracker crumbs and butter; press firmly on bottom of greased 13×9-inch baking pan.

3. In large bowl, beat cream cheese until fluffy. Gradually beat in EAGLE BRAND® until smooth. Add eggs, lemon juice and vanilla; mix well. Pour over crust.

4. Drop strawberry mixture by spoonfuls over batter. Gently swirl with knife or spatula. Bake 25 to 30 minutes or until center is set. Cool. Chill. Cut into bars. Store leftovers covered in refrigerator.

Prep Time: 20 minutes
Bake Time: 25 to 30 minutes

apple oatmeal spice cookies

Makes about 36 cookies

- ⅔ cup firmly packed brown sugar
- ¼ cup granulated sugar
- ¼ cup (½ stick) light butter, softened
- ¾ cup unsweetened applesauce or apple butter
- 1 egg
- 2 tablespoons fat-free (skim) milk
- 2 teaspoons vanilla
- 1½ cups all-purpose flour
- 1 teaspoon baking soda
- 1 teaspoon ground cinnamon
- ½ teaspoon salt (optional)
- ¼ teaspoon ground nutmeg (optional)
- 3 cups QUAKER® Oats (quick or old fashioned, uncooked)
- ¾ cup diced dried mixed fruit or raisins

1. Heat oven to 350°F. Lightly spray cookie sheets with nonstick cooking spray.

2. Beat sugars and butter in large bowl with electric mixer until well blended. Add applesauce, egg, milk and vanilla; beat well. Add combined flour, baking soda, cinnamon and, if desired, salt and nutmeg; mix well. Stir in oats and dried fruit; mix well. (Dough will be moist.)

3. Drop dough by rounded tablespoonfuls onto cookie sheets; press lightly to flatten.

4. Bake 12 to 14 minutes or until edges are light golden brown. Cool 1 minute on cookie sheets; remove to wire racks. Cool completely. Store tightly covered.

strawberry swirl cheesecake bars

banana oatmeal caramel cookies

Makes about 2 dozen cookies

1 package (16 ounces) refrigerated turtle cookie dough
2 ripe bananas, mashed
1⅓ cups old-fashioned oats
⅔ cup all-purpose flour
½ cup semisweet chocolate chips

1. Let dough stand at room temperature about 15 minutes. Preheat oven to 350°F. Lightly grease cookie sheets.

2. Beat dough, bananas, oats and flour in large bowl with electric mixer at medium speed until well blended. Drop dough by heaping tablespoonfuls 2 inches apart onto prepared cookie sheets; flatten slightly.

3. Bake 16 to 18 minutes or until edges are brown and centers are set. Cool on cookie sheets 1 minute. Remove to wire racks; cool completely.

4. Place chocolate chips in small resealable food storage bag. Microwave on MEDIUM (50%) 1 minute; knead bag lightly. Microwave and knead at additional 30-second intervals until chocolate is completely melted. Cut off tiny corner of bag. Drizzle melted chocolate over cookies. Let stand until set.

banana oatmeal caramel cookies

kahlúa® mudslide brownies

Makes about 2 dozen brownies

2 cups all-purpose flour
½ teaspoon baking powder
½ teaspoon salt
⅔ cup butter
4 squares (1 ounce each) unsweetened chocolate, chopped
3 eggs
1½ cups granulated sugar
4 tablespoons KAHLÚA® Liqueur
2 tablespoons Irish cream liqueur
1 tablespoon vodka
¾ cup coarsely chopped walnuts (optional)
KAHLÚA® Glaze (recipe follows)
Whole coffee beans (optional)

Preheat oven to 350°F. Combine flour, baking powder and salt in small bowl. Melt butter and chocolate in small saucepan over low heat; set aside. Beat eggs and granulated sugar in large bowl until light. Beat in flour mixture, chocolate mixture, 4 tablespoons Kahlúa®, Irish cream and vodka. Fold in walnuts. Pour into greased 13×9-inch baking pan.

Bake just until toothpick inserted into center comes out clean, about 25 minutes. *Do not overbake.* Cool in pan on wire rack. Spread with Kahlúa® Glaze. Decorate with whole coffee beans, if desired. Cut into squares.

kahlúa® glaze

1¼ cups powdered sugar
3 tablespoons KAHLÚA® Liqueur

Beat together powdered sugar and 3 tablespoons Kahlúa® in small bowl until smooth. *Makes about 1 cup*

chocolate cranberry bars

chocolate cranberry bars

Makes 36 bars

2 cups vanilla wafer crumbs
   (about 60 wafers, crushed)
½ cup HERSHEY'S Cocoa
3 tablespoons sugar
⅔ cup cold butter, cut into pieces
1 can (14 ounces) sweetened
   condensed milk (not evaporated
   milk)
1 cup REESE'S® Peanut Butter Chips
1⅓ cups (6-ounce package) sweetened
   dried cranberries *or* 1⅓ cups
   raisins
1 cup coarsely chopped walnuts

1. Heat oven to 350°F.

2. Stir together vanilla wafer crumbs, cocoa and sugar in medium bowl; cut in butter until crumbly. Press mixture evenly on bottom and ½ inch up sides of 13×9×2-inch baking pan. Pour sweetened condensed milk evenly over crumb mixture; sprinkle evenly with peanut butter chips and dried cranberries. Sprinkle nuts on top; press down firmly.

3. Bake 25 to 30 minutes or until lightly browned. Cool completely in pan on wire rack. Cover with foil; let stand several hours before cutting into bars and serving.

brown sugar cheesecake bars

Makes 18 servings

7 HONEY MAID® Honey Grahams, crushed
⅔ cup granulated sugar, divided
3 tablespoons butter, melted
2 packages (8 ounces each) PHILADELPHIA® Cream Cheese, softened
1 teaspoon vanilla
2 whole eggs
1 egg yolk
½ cup firmly packed brown sugar
1 tablespoon water

HEAT oven to 350°F. Mix graham crumbs, 2 tablespoons granulated sugar and butter. Press onto bottom of 9-inch square baking pan. Beat cream cheese, remaining granulated sugar and vanilla with electric mixer until blended. Add whole eggs and egg yolk; mix well. Pour over crust.

BAKE 30 minutes or until center is almost set. Cool completely. Refrigerate at least 3 hours.

HEAT broiler. Mix brown sugar and water; spread over cheesecake. Broil, 6 inches from heat, 1 minute or until topping is hot and bubbly. Serve warm.

Tip: Brown sugar is moist and clingy when fresh but can easily dry out and become hard as a rock. To soften brown sugar, place it in a microwavable bowl and cover with plastic wrap. Microwave on HIGH 30 to 45 seconds; stir and repeat if necessary.

walnut caramel triangles

Makes 4 dozen triangles

2 cups all-purpose flour
½ cup confectioners' sugar
1 cup (2 sticks) cold butter or margarine
1 (14-ounce) can EAGLE BRAND® Sweetened Condensed Milk (NOT evaporated milk)
½ cup whipping cream
1 teaspoon vanilla extract
1½ cups chopped walnuts
Chocolate Drizzle (recipe follows)

1. Preheat oven to 350°F. In medium bowl, combine flour and confectioners' sugar; cut in butter until crumbly. Press firmly on bottom of ungreased 13×9-inch baking pan. Bake 15 minutes or until lightly browned around edges.

2. In heavy saucepan over medium-high heat, combine EAGLE BRAND®, whipping cream and vanilla. Cook and stir until mixture comes to a boil. Reduce heat to medium; cook and stir until mixture thickens, 8 to 10 minutes. Stir in walnuts. Spread evenly over prepared crust.

3. Bake 20 minutes or until golden brown. Cool. Garnish with Chocolate Drizzle. Chill. Cut into triangles. Store leftovers covered at room temperature.

Chocolate Drizzle: Melt ½ cup semisweet chocolate chips with 1 teaspoon shortening. Carefully drizzle on with a spoon while warm.

Prep Time: 20 minutes
Bake Time: 35 minutes

chewy drizzled cinnamon chip cookies

chewy drizzled cinnamon chip cookies

Makes about 5 dozen cookies

¾ cup (1½ sticks) butter or
    margarine, softened
1 cup packed light brown sugar
¼ cup light corn syrup
1 egg
1⅔ cups (10-ounce package)
    HERSHEY₆S Cinnamon Chips,
    divided
2½ cups all-purpose flour
2 teaspoons baking soda
¼ teaspoon salt
1 cup finely ground pecans or
    walnuts
Cinnamon Chips Drizzle
    (recipe follows)

1. Beat butter and brown sugar in large bowl until fluffy. Add corn syrup and egg; mix well.

2. Place 1 cup cinnamon chips in microwave-safe bowl. Microwave at MEDIUM (50%) 1 minute; stir. If necessary, microwave at MEDIUM an additional 15 seconds at a time, stirring after each heating, just until chips are melted when stirred. Stir melted chips into butter mixture.

3. Stir together flour, baking soda and salt; add to cinnamon chips mixture, beating just until blended. Cover; refrigerate dough about 1 hour or until firm enough to handle.

4. Heat oven to 350°F. Shape dough into 1-inch balls; roll in nuts, lightly pressing nuts into dough. Place on ungreased cookie sheet.

5. Bake 8 to 10 minutes or until golden around edges. Cool slightly; remove from cookie sheet to wire rack. Cool completely. Drizzle with Cinnamon Chips Drizzle.

Cinnamon Chips Drizzle: Place remaining ⅔ cup cinnamon chips and 1½ teaspoons shortening (do not use butter, margarine, spread or oil) in small microwave-safe bowl. Microwave at MEDIUM (50%) 1 minute; stir until chips are melted and mixture is smooth.

butterscotch spice cookies

Makes 3 dozen cookies

1 package DUNCAN HINES®
    Moist Deluxe® Spice Cake Mix
2 eggs
½ cup vegetable oil
1 teaspoon vanilla extract
1 cup butterscotch flavored chips

1. Preheat oven to 375°F.

2. Combine cake mix, eggs, oil and vanilla extract in large bowl. Beat at low speed with electric mixer until blended. Stir in butterscotch chips. Drop by rounded teaspoonfuls 2 inches apart onto ungreased baking sheets. Bake at 375°F for 8 to 10 minutes or until set. Cool 2 minutes on baking sheets. Remove to cooling racks. Cool completely. Store in airtight container.

rocky road brownies

Makes 2 dozen brownies

Brownie
- ½ cup butter or margarine
- 3 ounces unsweetened baking chocolate
- 1 cup all-purpose flour
- ¾ teaspoon baking powder
- ½ teaspoon salt
- 3 eggs
- 1½ cups DOMINO® Granulated Sugar
- 1½ teaspoons vanilla

Topping
- ½ cup chopped peanuts
- ½ cup semi-sweet chocolate chips
- ½ cup miniature marshmallows
- ¼ cup chocolate fudge topping, warmed

Heat oven to 350°F. Generously grease 9-inch square baking pan. Melt butter and unsweetened chocolate over low heat in medium saucepan, stirring frequently; cool. Combine flour, baking powder and salt in small bowl; set aside.

Beat eggs in large bowl until light. Add sugar, 2 tablespoons at a time, beating until mixture is thick. Add vanilla. Gradually add chocolate mixture to egg mixture. Stir in flour mixture just until blended. Spread evenly in prepared pan.

Bake at 350°F for 25 to 30 minutes or until edges pull away from sides of pan slightly. Remove from oven. Sprinkle peanuts, chocolate chips and marshmallows over top; drizzle with chocolate fudge topping. Continue baking 8 to 12 minutes or until lightly browned. Cool completely. Cut into bars.

Prep Time: 30 minutes
Bake Time: 42 minutes

nutmeg molasses cookies

Makes about 5 dozen cookies

- 1½ cups sugar
- 1 cup shortening
- ⅓ cup molasses
- 1 teaspoon vanilla
- 2 eggs
- 3 cups all-purpose flour
- 2 teaspoons baking soda
- 1 teaspoon ground nutmeg
- 1 teaspoon ground cinnamon
- ½ teaspoon salt

1. Preheat oven to 350°F.

2. Beat sugar, shortening, molasses and vanilla in large bowl with electric mixer at medium speed until creamy. Add eggs, one at a time, beating well after each addition.

3. Combine flour, baking soda, nutmeg, cinnamon and salt in medium bowl; gradually add to shortening mixture, beating at low speed until blended. Beat at medium speed until thick dough forms.

4. Shape dough into 1½-inch balls. Place 3 inches apart on ungreased cookie sheets. Flatten with bottom of glass dipped in sugar.

5. Bake 10 minutes or until cookies look dry. Cool completely on wire racks.

nutmeg molasses cookies

chocolatey raspberry crumb bars

Makes 3 dozen bars

- 1 cup (2 sticks) butter or margarine, softened
- 2 cups all-purpose flour
- ½ cup packed light brown sugar
- ¼ teaspoon salt
- 2 cups (12-ounce package) NESTLÉ® TOLL HOUSE® Semi-Sweet Chocolate Morsels, *divided*
- 1 can (14 ounces) NESTLÉ® CARNATION® Sweetened Condensed Milk
- ½ cup chopped nuts (optional)
- ⅓ cup seedless raspberry jam

PREHEAT oven to 350°F. Grease 13×9-inch baking pan.

BEAT butter in large mixer bowl until creamy. Beat in flour, sugar and salt until crumbly. With floured fingers, press *1¾ cups* crumb mixture onto bottom of prepared baking pan; reserve *remaining* mixture.

BAKE for 10 to 12 minutes or until edges are golden brown.

MICROWAVE *1 cup* morsels and sweetened condensed milk in medium, uncovered, microwave-safe bowl on HIGH (100%) power for 1 minute. STIR. Morsels may retain some of their original shape. If necessary, microwave at additional 10- to 15-second intervals, stirring just until morsels are melted. Spread over hot crust.

STIR nuts into *reserved* crumb mixture; sprinkle over chocolate layer. Drop teaspoonfuls of raspberry jam over crumb mixture. Sprinkle with *remaining* morsels.

BAKE for 25 to 30 minutes or until center is set. Cool in pan on wire rack. Cut into bars.

peanut butter & jelly thumbprint cookies

Makes 4 dozen cookies

- 3 cups all-purpose flour
- 1½ teaspoons baking powder
- ½ teaspoon salt
- 1 cup SHEDD'S SPREAD COUNTRY CROCK® Spread
- ½ cup granulated sugar
- ½ cup firmly packed light brown sugar
- ½ cup SKIPPY® Creamy Peanut Butter
- 1 egg
- 1½ teaspoons vanilla extract
- ¼ cup grape jelly

1. In medium bowl, combine flour, baking powder and salt; set aside.

2. In large bowl, with electric mixer, beat Spread, sugars and SKIPPY® Creamy Peanut Butter until light and fluffy, about 3 minutes. Beat in egg and vanilla, scraping sides occasionally. Gradually beat in flour mixture until blended. Wrap dough in plastic wrap and freeze at least 1 hour.

3. Preheat oven to 425°F. On ungreased baking sheets, shape by tablespoonfuls into balls and arrange. With thumb or rounded ¼ teaspoon measure, make indentation in center of each cookie; fill each with ¼ teaspoon jelly.

4. Bake 5 minutes or until bottoms of cookies are lightly golden. On wire rack, cool completely.

Prep Time: 15 minutes
Chill Time: 1 hour
Cook Time: 5 minutes

chocolatey raspberry crumb bars

triple peanut butter oatmeal bars

triple peanut butter oatmeal bars

Makes 32 bars

1½ cups firmly packed brown sugar
1 cup peanut butter
½ cup (1 stick) margarine or butter, softened
2 large eggs
1 teaspoon vanilla
2 cups QUAKER® Oats (quick or old fashioned, uncooked)
1 cup all-purpose flour
½ teaspoon baking soda
1 bag (8 ounces) candy-coated peanut butter pieces
½ cup chopped peanuts

1. Heat oven to 350°F. Lightly spray 13×9-inch baking pan with nonstick cooking spray.

2. Beat brown sugar, peanut butter and margarine in large bowl with electric mixer until creamy. Add eggs and vanilla; beat well. Add combined oats, flour and baking soda; mix well. Stir in peanut butter pieces. Spread dough evenly into pan. Sprinkle with peanuts, pressing in lightly with fingers.

3. Bake 35 to 40 minutes or just until center is set. Cool completely on wire rack. Cut into bars. Store tightly covered.

banana split cheesecake squares

Makes 18 servings

2 cups HONEY MAID® Graham Cracker Crumbs
⅓ cup butter or margarine, melted
1 cup sugar, divided
3 packages (8 ounces each) PHILADELPHIA® Cream Cheese, softened
1 teaspoon vanilla
3 eggs
½ cup mashed banana
1 cup halved strawberries
1 banana, sliced, tossed with 1 teaspoon lemon juice
1 can (8 ounces) pineapple chunks, drained

MIX graham crumbs, butter and ¼ cup of sugar. Press onto bottom of 13×9-inch baking pan.

MIX cream cheese, remaining ¾ cup of sugar and vanilla with electric mixer on medium speed until well blended. Add eggs; mix just until blended. Stir in mashed banana. Pour into crust.

BAKE at 350°F for 30 minutes or until center is almost set. Cool. Refrigerate 3 hours or overnight.

TOP with strawberries, sliced banana and pineapple. Cut into squares.

Special Extra: Prepare and refrigerate as directed. Sprinkle with ¼ cup finely chopped PLANTERS® Pecans and drizzle with melted BAKER'S® Semi-Sweet Baking Chocolate before cutting into squares.

Prep Time: 20 minutes
Total Time: 3 hours 50 minutes

zesty fresh lemon bars

Makes about 3 dozen bars

Crust
- ½ cup butter or margarine, softened
- ½ cup granulated sugar
- Grated peel of ½ SUNKIST® lemon
- 1¼ cups all-purpose flour

Filling
- 1 cup packed brown sugar
- 1 cup chopped walnuts
- 2 eggs, slightly beaten
- ¼ cup all-purpose flour
- Grated peel of ½ SUNKIST® lemon
- ¼ teaspoon baking powder

Glaze
- 1 cup powdered sugar
- 1 tablespoon butter or margarine, softened
- 2 tablespoons fresh-squeezed SUNKIST® lemon juice

To prepare crust, preheat oven to 350°F. In medium bowl, beat ½ cup butter, granulated sugar and lemon peel. Gradually stir in 1¼ cups flour to form soft dough. Press evenly on bottom of ungreased 13×9×2-inch pan. Bake 15 minutes.

To prepare filling, in medium bowl, combine all filling ingredients. Spread over baked crust. Bake 20 minutes. Meanwhile, prepare glaze.

To prepare glaze, in small bowl, gradually blend small amount of powdered sugar into 1 tablespoon butter. Add lemon juice and remaining powdered sugar; stir to blend well. Drizzle glaze over hot filling. Cool in pan on wire rack; cut into bars. Store tightly covered at room temperature.

double chip brownies

Makes about 36 brownies

- ¾ cup HERSHEY'S Cocoa
- ½ teaspoon baking soda
- ⅔ cup butter or margarine, melted and divided
- ½ cup boiling water
- 2 cups sugar
- 2 eggs
- 1⅓ cups all-purpose flour
- 1 teaspoon vanilla extract
- ¼ teaspoon salt
- 1 cup HERSHEY'S Milk Chocolate Chips
- 1 cup REESE'S® Peanut Butter Chips

1. Heat oven to 350°F. Grease 13×9-inch baking pan.

2. Stir together cocoa and baking soda in large bowl; stir in ⅓ cup melted butter. Add boiling water; stir until mixture thickens. Stir in sugar, eggs and remaining ⅓ cup melted butter; stir until smooth. Add flour, vanilla and salt; blend thoroughly. Stir in milk chocolate chips and peanut butter chips. Spread in prepared pan.

3. Bake 35 to 40 minutes or until brownies begin to pull away from sides of pan. Cool completely in pan on wire rack. Cut into squares.

double chip brownies

chocolate & malt bars

Makes 2 dozen bars

1 cup all-purpose flour
1 cup malted milk powder or malted
   milk drink mix
2 teaspoons baking powder
¼ teaspoon salt
½ cup granulated sugar
¼ cup firmly packed light brown sugar
¼ cup (½ stick) butter, softened
½ cup milk
½ teaspoon vanilla extract
2 large eggs
1 cup "M&M's"® Chocolate Mini
   Baking Bits, divided
   Chocolate Malt Frosting
   (recipe follows)

Preheat oven to 350°F. Lightly grease
13×9-inch baking pan; set aside. In
large bowl combine flour, malted milk
powder, baking powder and salt; stir in
sugars. Beat in butter, milk and vanilla;
blend well. Add eggs; beat 2 minutes.
Spread batter in prepared pan. Sprinkle
with ¼ cup "M&M's"® Chocolate Mini
Baking Bits. Bake about 20 minutes or
until toothpick inserted in center comes
out clean. Cool completely on wire rack.
Prepare Chocolate Malt Frosting; spread
over cake. Sprinkle with remaining
¾ cup "M&M's"® Chocolate Mini
Baking Bits. Store in tightly covered
container.

chocolate malt frosting

¼ cup (½ stick) butter, softened
4 teaspoons light corn syrup
½ teaspoon vanilla extract
¼ cup malted milk powder or malted
   milk drink mix
3 tablespoons unsweetened cocoa
   powder
1½ cups powdered sugar
3 to 4 tablespoons milk

In small bowl beat butter, corn syrup
and vanilla; add malted milk powder
and cocoa powder until well blended.
Blend in powdered sugar and enough
milk for good spreading consistency.
Makes about 2 cups

strawberry pecan jumbles

Makes 18 bars

1¼ cups all-purpose flour
½ cup CREAM OF WHEAT® Hot
   Cereal (Instant, 1-minute,
   2½-minute or 10-minute
   cook time), uncooked
⅓ cup chopped pecans
⅓ cup sugar
½ teaspoon baking powder
½ cup (1 stick) butter or margarine,
   melted
1 egg, lightly beaten
1 teaspoon vanilla extract
½ cup POLANER® All Fruit®
   Strawberry Fruit Spread

1. Preheat oven to 375°F. Lightly grease
9-inch square baking pan.

2. Blend flour, Cream of Wheat, pecans,
sugar and baking powder in large bowl.
Stir in butter, egg and vanilla until
crumbly. Reserve ½ cup mixture.

3. Press remaining Cream of Wheat
mixture on bottom of prepared baking
pan. Smooth fruit spread evenly over
bottom; crumble reserved mixture over
fruit spread.

4. Bake 18 to 20 minutes or until golden
brown. Cool completely in pan on wire
rack. Cut into bars.

Prep Time: 15 minutes
Start-to-Finish Time: 35 minutes

chocolate chip chocolate cookies

Makes about 3½ dozen cookies

½ cup (1 stick) butter or margarine, softened
1 cup sugar
1 egg
1 teaspoon vanilla extract
1½ cups all-purpose flour
⅓ cup HERSHEY'S Cocoa
½ teaspoon baking soda
½ teaspoon salt
¼ cup milk
1 cup HERSHEY'S SPECIAL DARK® Chocolate Chips or HERSHEY'S Semi-Sweet Chocolate Chips

1. Heat oven to 375°F.

2. Beat butter, sugar, egg and vanilla in large bowl until fluffy. Combine flour, cocoa, baking soda and salt; add alternately with milk to butter mixture, blending well. Stir in chocolate chips. Drop by rounded teaspoons onto ungreased cookie sheets.

3. Bake 8 to 10 minutes or until set. *Do not overbake.* Cool 1 minute. Remove from cookie sheets; cool completely on wire racks.

dulce de leche blondies

dulce de leche blondies

Makes about 3 dozen bars

2 cups all-purpose flour
1 teaspoon baking soda
1 teaspoon salt
1 cup (2 sticks) butter, softened
1 cup firmly packed brown sugar
2 eggs
1½ teaspoons vanilla
1 (14-ounce) package caramels
½ cup evaporated milk

1. Preheat oven to 350°F. Grease 13×9-inch baking pan. Sift flour, baking soda and salt into medium bowl.

2. Beat butter and brown sugar in large bowl with electric mixer at medium speed until creamy. Add eggs and vanilla; beat until smooth. Gradually stir in flour mixture. Spread half of batter in prepared pan. Bake 8 minutes. Cool in pan 5 minutes.

3. Meanwhile, melt caramels with evaporated milk in nonstick saucepan over very low heat; reserve 2 tablespoons. Pour remaining caramel over baked bottom layer. Drop tablespoonfuls of remaining batter over caramel layer; swirl slightly with knife.

4. Bake 25 minutes or until golden brown. Cool completely in pan on wire rack. Cut into squares. Reheat reserved caramel, if necessary; drizzle over bars.

pecan florentines

Makes about 3 dozen cookies

¾ cup pecan halves, finely ground*
½ cup all-purpose flour
⅓ cup packed brown sugar
¼ cup light corn syrup
¼ cup (½ stick) butter
2 tablespoons milk
⅓ cup semisweet chocolate chips

To grind pecans, place in food processor or blender. Process until thoroughly ground with a dry, not pasty, texture.

1. Preheat oven to 350°F. Line cookie sheets with foil; lightly grease foil. Combine pecans and flour in small bowl. Combine brown sugar, corn syrup, butter and milk in medium saucepan. Cook and stir over medium heat until mixture comes to a boil. Remove from heat; stir in flour mixture.

2. Drop by teaspoonfuls about 3 inches apart onto prepared cookie sheets. Bake 10 to 12 minutes or until lacy and golden brown. (Cookies will become crisp as they cool.) Cool completely on foil.

3. Place chocolate chips in small resealable food storage bag; seal. Microwave on HIGH 30 seconds. Knead bag lightly. Repeat as necessary until chips are completely melted. Cut off small corner from bag. Drizzle melted chocolate over cookies. Let stand until chocolate is set. Peel cookies off foil.

Tip: Silicone mats make the job of baking florentines a breeze. Their surface allows the cookies to peel right off without breaking or tearing, and they don't require nonstick cooking spray or oil. They come in many different sizes to fit most baking sheets.

pecan florentines

snow-covered almond crescents

Makes 5 dozen cookies

1 package (8 ounces) PHILADELPHIA® Cream Cheese, softened
¾ cup (1½ sticks) butter, softened
1 cup granulated sugar
2 teaspoons vanilla
½ teaspoon almond extract
2¼ cups all-purpose flour
½ teaspoon baking soda
1 cup finely chopped PLANTERS® Slivered Almonds
¾ cup powdered sugar

BEAT first 5 ingredients in large bowl with electric mixer until well blended. Add flour and baking soda; mix well. Stir in nuts. Refrigerate 30 minutes.

HEAT oven to 350°F. Roll dough into 60 (1-inch) balls; shape each into crescent shape. Place, 2 inches apart, on baking sheets. Flatten slightly.

BAKE 10 to 12 minutes or until lightly browned. Cool 3 minutes on baking sheets; transfer to wire racks. Cool completely; sprinkle with powdered sugar.

Pecan Crescents: Substitute finely chopped PLANTERS® Pecans for the almonds.

metric conversion chart

· · · · ·

VOLUME MEASUREMENTS (dry)

⅛ teaspoon = 0.5 mL
¼ teaspoon = 1 mL
½ teaspoon = 2 mL
¾ teaspoon = 4 mL
1 teaspoon = 5 mL
1 tablespoon = 15 mL
2 tablespoons = 30 mL
¼ cup = 60 mL
⅓ cup = 75 mL
½ cup = 125 mL
⅔ cup = 150 mL
¾ cup = 175 mL
1 cup = 250 mL
2 cups = 1 pint = 500 mL
3 cups = 750 mL
4 cups = 1 quart = 1 L

VOLUME MEASUREMENTS (fluid)

1 fluid ounce (2 tablespoons) = 30 mL
4 fluid ounces (½ cup) = 125 mL
8 fluid ounces (1 cup) = 250 mL
12 fluid ounces (1½ cups) = 375 mL
16 fluid ounces (2 cups) = 500 mL

WEIGHTS (mass)

½ ounce = 15 g
1 ounce = 30 g
3 ounces = 90 g
4 ounces = 120 g
8 ounces = 225 g
10 ounces = 285 g
12 ounces = 360 g
16 ounces = 1 pound = 450 g

DIMENSIONS

1/16 inch = 2 mm
⅛ inch = 3 mm
¼ inch = 6 mm
½ inch = 1.5 cm
¾ inch = 2 cm
1 inch = 2.5 cm

OVEN TEMPERATURES

250°F = 120°C
275°F = 140°C
300°F = 150°C
325°F = 160°C
350°F = 180°C
375°F = 190°C
400°F = 200°C
425°F = 220°C
450°F = 230°C

BAKING PAN SIZES

Utensil	Size in Inches/Quarts	Metric Volume	Size in Centimeters
Baking or Cake Pan (square or rectangular)	8×8×2	2 L	20×20×5
	9×9×2	2.5 L	23×23×5
	12×8×2	3 L	30×20×5
	13×9×2	3.5 L	33×23×5
Loaf Pan	8×4×3	1.5 L	20×10×7
	9×5×3	2 L	23×13×7
Round Layer Cake Pan	8×1½	1.2 L	20×4
	9×1½	1.5 L	23×4
Pie Plate	8×1¼	750 mL	20×3
	9×1¼	1 L	23×3
Baking Dish or Casserole	1 quart	1 L	—
	1½ quart	1.5 L	—
	2 quart	2 L	—

seasonal celebrations